Groupwork in Social Care

Julie Phillips

Jessica Kingsley Publishers
London and Philadelphia

First published in the United Kingdom in 2001 by
Jessica Kingsley Publishers Ltd
116 Pentonville Road
London N1 9JB, England
and
325 Chestnut Street
Philadelphia, PA 19106, USA

www.jkp.com

Copyright © 2001 Julie Phillips

Library of Congress Cataloging in Publication Data
A CIP catalog record for this book is available from the Library of Congress

British Library Cataloguing in Publication Data
A CIP catalogue record for this book is available from the British Library

ISBN 1 85302 829 0

Printed and Bound in Great Britain by
Athenaeum Press, Gateshead, Tyne and Wear

To Professor Maurice Broady, whose pedagogic example I hope
I echo with my own students, with affection and thanks

Contents

Preface

While increasing attention is being paid to the use of groupwork to meet core activity in human services agencies, groupwork literature, although expanding into more specialist areas, continues to focus mainly on groupwork dynamics once a group is in process. This book's purpose is to explore some of the issues which face caring professionals in the initial planning stages of setting up a group. A number of complex processes need to be considered before the essential areas of decision making are completed, so that a group can begin to operate with the best chance of success. 'Research evidence and practice experience both testify that effectiveness or success are determined as much by what happens before the group comes into existence, as by what happens during the group's life' (Brown 1994, p.34).

The prevalence of groupwork in human services agencies was perhaps at its height in the 1970s. In succeeding years some agencies' priorities changed and groupwork was viewed by some managers as a luxury rather than being central to meeting core agency activity. Partly in response to a range of factors, such as changes in legislation for adults and older people and the search for more effective initiatives in health, child care and offenders' agencies, there has been recently a growth in agencies initiating groupwork programmes to provide core services. This is particularly so in health-related areas, children's agencies where there is a growth in 'positive parenting' groups, and probation services where groupwork with sex offenders is seen as a very effective approach. This growth means that some workers new to groupwork are now expected to grasp a set of unfamiliar skills and provide groupwork responses which perhaps their agency has not itself previously used.

Groupwork is a professional tool in a range of human services agencies in the statutory, voluntary and private sectors. This book focuses on the planning needs of group workers in these agencies as well as in professional groups which have traditionally practised groupwork: youth workers, occupational therapists, community mental health nurses, psychotherapists and social workers.

Chapter 1 presents an historical overview of the development of groupwork across a range of agency and multidisciplinary contexts, together with a perspective on current provision. Several frameworks are provided in an exploration of the utility to the practitioner of trying to categorize groups. These include: group characteristics, group purposes and theoretical frameworks.

The book's practice core is provided by the eight case studies in Chapter 2. These illustrate the preparation and decision-making processes in a range of groups in their initial planning phases. These include groups in the voluntary and statutory sectors and represent a range of professional workers and client groups. Succeeding chapters draw on these practice examples to explore the dilemmas facing practitioners in their planning tasks.

The third chapter explores some of the central issues around power, race and gender in groupwork. These are clearly issues which must be considered in relation to all the planning aspects of any group. Race, gender and other aspects of anti-oppressive practice are considered particularly in relation to the selection of group members, and leadership and co-leadership. Since four of the practice groups are single-gender groups, some of the theoretical elements introduced in this chapter have very practical applications.

Chapter 4 is devoted to group goals. The process by which overarching group goals emerge is sometimes complex and certainly infinitely varied between different groups. The extent to which group workers have goals for individual members, whether overt or covert, is equally varied. The case study groups amply illustrate these differences.

The importance of the group's physical environment is explored in Chapter 5. This chapter asserts that practitioners in planning groups should, where possible, consciously plan the environment as part of the groupwork experience for members and acknowledge the contribution of the environment to the achievement of group goals. Groupwork literature, environmental psychology and the concerns of group workers are utilized to pursue a number of dimensions of this often-neglected topic.

Chapter 6 concerns group programmes and group activities. The case study groups are used to focus on how professionals select or reject activities for groups at the planning stage. Consideration is given to assessing whether the criteria for the selection of activities relates to the achievement of group goals. There is a focus on the types of activities most generally salient in groups run by particular professions and on the author's use of an activity analysis framework applied to groupwork in a mental health day centre.

Group structure and its relationship to successful group outcomes are analysed in Chapter 7. Although leadership issues are clearly a central part of initial planning decisions for practitioners, this area is not included here since it is covered in considerable detail elsewhere (Benson 1987; Brown 1994; Douglas 1976, 1978, 1983, 1991; Preston-Shoot 1987).

The intended utility of this book for practitioners lies in the demonstration of theoretical issues in the planning dilemmas of the case study groups and their workers. The contribution of these group workers therefore has been essential to the writing of this book. I should like to thank the following practice colleagues who gave me their time and who were prepared to share their personal groupwork experiences: Chris Bromhall, Amelia Gentles, Anne Green, Sandra Kiernan, Judith McCarthy, Geraldine McGill, Maggie Mills, Amelia Taylor, Stephanie Smith and Moira Sugden. A large number of academic colleagues from a range of qualifying programmes in the caring services also gave me their time and help. In particular I give my thanks to: Hilary Johnson, University College Northampton, Mary Tyler, De Montfort University, and Sue Waters, Coventry University.

J.P.

Chapter 1

The Groupwork Context

Groupwork in the UK, although it did not begin to emerge in its present form until the 1940s, had some of its antecedent history in the nineteenth century (Kuenstler 1954). These foundations lie in inner-city initiatives which emanated from the voluntary sector and which were particularly focused on the needs of young people. Such initiatives include the YMCA and the Scout movements, the foundations of the present youth services and the growth of inner-city settlements. Later the Outward Bound movement emerged (Fletcher 1970). In the USA similar initiatives for young people developed into a recognized professional groupwork forum.

In the UK such professional development in groupwork was much slower. In the 1940s social workers and mental health practitioners began to view groupwork as a means of making greater use of members' own resources. Heap (1985) suggests that these early workers recognized that groupwork could raise self-esteem, and that solutions and coping strategies suggested by group members in their own situation were more powerful than those suggested by professionals. In the late 1940s, but more particularly in the 1950s and 1960s, group psychotherapy grew from its base in psychiatry. Skynner, in his Foreword to Dwivedi (1993), tells us that while in psychiatry training he worked with a colleague who was experimenting with group psychotherapy with children. Later, in the 1950s and 1960s, Skynner developed group psychotherapy for children as a mode of treatment in several UK child guidance clinics. 'I was soon running about eight a week, while a colleague added to that number' (Foreword, Dwivedi 1993). Clearly the establishment of multidisciplinary child guidance clinics provided the context for a wide range of groups for children and families. These were based on a number of theoretical frameworks, including family therapy, and behavioural and psychodynamic approaches.

In the 1960s and early 1970s, as groupwork grew in the UK, practitioners had to draw heavily on American literature. Here the developed body of professional knowledge and practice had produced a range of excellent literature (Hare 1962; Hartford 1972; Konopka 1963; Vinter 1967; Whittaker 1974). In the UK, although there was some earlier groupwork literature (Churchill 1959; Parsloe 1968), the broad growth of groupwork literature began in the 1970s (Brown 1979; Davies 1975; Douglas 1970, 1976; Heap 1979). Throughout the 1970s and 1980s a very broad range of groupwork continued to grow.

In these decades community work was seen as a separate profession with its own training programmes. Community work was also usually a core element of most social work courses so that some community workers would be recruited from this source. The predominant ideologies of this sector had a different focus from the other caring professions of this period. There was a clear element of empowering and providing consultation for existing community groups and of aiding in the formation of tenants and single-issue campaign groups. Community workers were also involved, as well as probation and social services departments, in the running of intermediate treatment groups. These groups were run for young people, some but not all of whom would be subject by the court to an intermediate treatment order. They were long-term groups which lasted between one and four years. During this period groupwork flourished in the probation service. Typical groups might be anger management, use of alcohol and facing up to offending behaviour. Occupational therapists, by this time, were clearly seen as providing groupwork in hospital units and day hospitals. They provided groupwork for a very broad range of users, including older people with memory difficulties and psychodrama for young people with mental health problems. This profession, together with social workers, are very evidently part of the multidisciplinary approach to groupwork of this period. An ongoing psychotherapy group run in the outpatients department of a psychiatric hospital was run by an occupational therapist, a clinical psychologist and a psychiatrist in training, while a social skills group was run by a social worker and a clinical psychologist. Medical settings groups usually included a range of professional workers, while social services groups more usually included social work practitioners. In parallel to these developments, groupwork was also well embedded in professional practice in the voluntary sector: family service units and Mind were particularly active here.

At the present time, some of the above trends continue. A range of professions in the human services continue to work together as co-workers and all these professions continue to develop a range of groupwork initiatives. Some examples are provided in Chapter 2 and discussed in the following chapters. Structural changes to the context of some of the agencies have changed some aspects of groupwork and may well change them further in the future. The reduction in the functions of social services departments is obviously strengthening the voluntary sector. Groupwork is currently very strong in a number of voluntary children's agencies; for example, the NCH and NSPCC. There is a continued growth in substance misuse agencies in both the health and voluntary sectors. It seems likely that there will be continued growth in groupwork as this sector expands. In the statutory sector, the probation service continues to use groupwork as a professional tool. The 1990 Community Care Act and subsequent policy directives may well encourage the trend of caring professionals from a range of disciplines in statutory agencies co-operating to jointly organize groupwork. The Anxiety Management Group in Chapter 2 has an occupational therapist and the Women's Mental Health Group is organized by a community mental health nurse and an occupational therapist. The Kingfisher Project, a groupwork initiative for bereaved children, has been developed in the North West Health Region by a multidisciplinary group of workers from health, education, social services and the voluntary sector. This is a relatively new and underdeveloped area (Williams *et al.* 1998). The youth service, within local education departments, now provides much of the groupwork for 13 to 25 year olds. A proportion of this provision is project based with short-term funding, and is often run in partnership with schools, social services departments and a range of voluntary organizations. These provide not only the more traditional neighbourhood youth clubs but also groups for mothers under 16, conciliation services on race issues in local contexts, groups for unemployed young people, support systems for young sex workers and projects for young people excluded from school. The new interdisciplinary approach to young people's services may well additionally increase the number of groupwork initiatives in this sector, in parallel to similar initiatives which resulted from the introduction of intermediate treatment groups in the 1970s. Lloyd and Maas (1997) suggest that occupational therapists in psychiatric hospital settings found organizing groupwork in a ward environment very frustrating. This is thought to be a response to the changing structure of hospital stays, which are now often considerably shorter. Peloquin (1983) states that occupational therapists working in acute psychiatric settings are expected to maximize therapy within a limited time-frame.

Why do groupwork?

It seems evident that, in the human services, group work has become, over a number of decades, a generally accepted strategy for improving the quality of life of people in a very broad range of situations. Groupwork is now one of the professional tools available to youth workers, occupational therapists, nurses, social workers, community workers and many other workers in social welfare agencies. Given that the main focus of training of most of the groups of professionals currently engaged in groupwork is on individual intervention, why do they view groupwork as an effective approach?

Heap (1985) suggests that the use of groups 'so often increases the quality and the relevance of help' (p.9). He states that this is because group members help themselves and other members by sharing information and feelings, comparing attitudes and experiences and developing relationships with each other. Heap says that these are basic human tendencies and as such the group worker needs to acknowledge the primacy of the group processes as the main resource in groupwork.

For Coulshed and Orme (1998) the utility of groupwork is its capacity to bring about change. Group membership is seen to encourage participants to disclose aspects of their own lives and behaviours and to give feedback to others on how their behaviour and responses affects group members or the wider context such as their families, employers or neighbours. The growth of this insight into personal motivation and others' reactions is seen as providing good potential for change. The type of change achieved is also seen to be more lasting because it embodies generalizable coping skills. The essence of the utility of groupwork for Coulshed and Orme (1998) and Heap (1985) is that it utilizes the personal resources of members to ameliorate concerns and provides a capacity 'to help as well as be helped' (Coulshed and Orme 1998, p.196). However, these authors do not underestimate the complex nature of group dynamics and both devote space to encouraging workers to gain appropriate skills.

What is a group?

Most groupwork writers give some attention to this question, much of it of little utility to the reader. This is because their definitions usually try to encompass all forms of human groups from the family to specific, time-limited treatment groups. Brown (1994), Douglas (1995) and Preston-Shoot (1987), while retaining sufficient breadth to include a very broad range of groups, provide criteria of use to groupwork practitioners.

In order to be described as a group, Preston-Shoot (1987) thinks that the members should have a shared purpose, be interdependent, have some physical proximity, retain some recognition of group boundaries and exist within a range of time-frames, although not to continue indefinitely. Brown (1994) provides similiar criteria. He suggests that the key concepts are: a defined membership; interdependence; boundaries; agreed purpose; and some size limitations – for example, no more than 12 members. Douglas's (1995) essential criteria for a group is that members 'have some need however tenuous of each other' (p.15). Douglas develops this theme of member dependence and is supported by most groupwork writers in viewing this element as core to an understanding of groupwork practice. Douglas continues his groupwork criteria by providing a table which classifies groups by various criteria (Table 1.1).

Table 1.1 Types and purposes of groups

Criteria	Classification	Characteristics
1. Nature	Natural/Artificial	Familiarity and tradition/Novelty and suspicion
2. Origin	Created/ Spontaneous	Conscious intent/Generation by pressure of circumstances
3. Leader	Directive/ Non-directive	Different ideas of the basis of enduring change in human beings
4. Location	Environmental influences	The ethos, structure and management of the organization in which a group is embedded (e.g. hospital, school, etc.)
5. Members	Selection criteria	Principal characteristics of group members (e.g. age, gender, race, problem, availability)
6. Outcome	Group purpose	What the group is set up or adapted to achieve (e.g. learning, support, change, etc.)
7. Number	Size	The effect of large/small groups
8. Throughput	Open/Closed	Whether group membership remains the same throughout the life of the group or not
9. Orientation	Approach	The selected theory base of the organization/leader/writer
10. Programme	Choice of activity	The principal activity used in the group (e.g. talk, drama, work, discussion, mixed, etc.)
11. Duration	Time factor	The length of group sessions or the length of time the group exists

Source: Douglas (1995, p.16)

Douglas (1995) emphasizes that all group characteristics are interrelated so that a change in one principal characteristic will have some effect on others; for example, a group that moves from being a mainly recreational group for socially isolated mothers to a group providing parenting skills may well change a number of its characteristics. Here the group outcome or purpose has changed. Such a group may have been self-directed; that is, managed without a worker or formal leader but by the group members themselves. Its new purpose may well necessitate a leader or leaders, perhaps a closed membership, and perhaps a change in time duration. It has clearly changed the orientation in that the group's theoretical base may well now be behavioural, and the programme is likely to change from perhaps general discussion to monitored exercises.

Another useful classification of groups is provided by Preston-Shoot (1987, p.11). He describes nine categories of groups. These however are not mutually exclusive, in that elements of one type can be found in another. The nine categories are briefly summarized here:

1. *Social groups.* The purpose may be to overcome members' social isolation, provide opportunities for pleasure or positive relationships. The content is social or recreational. Group workers may be responsible for the programme or members may be wholly or partly responsible. Examples of social groups are youth clubs, social clubs for older people, social clubs for people with learning disabilities.

2. *Group psychotherapy.* The purpose is usually to effect basic personality change through individual goals. Members are likely to bring a whole range of personal problems and interpersonal coping difficulties. They rely on good verbal communication skills of members. The group is oriented towards present events in the group. Members need to find psychological explanations acceptable. The orientation towards present group behaviour is intended to help people to change by recognizing how they relate to others in the group. Bion (1961) and Yalom (1975, 1985) are major contributors to this field.

3. *Group counselling.* Usually members share a common problem which is the focus for the group. This may be practical, such as completing a well-presented curriculum vitae, or be emotional or interpersonal. The group workers' tasks are to help members clarify the problem, share solutions and develop problem-solving behaviours.

4. *Educational groups.* The purpose is to provide information and to impart skills. Two types of groups are included: (a) practical skills – could be daily living skills or negotiating skills with social welfare agencies; (b) preparing people for life stages such as transitions from work to retirement, the adoption of a child, or junior to secondary school. The group content may include some information giving but the main emphasis is on learning transferable skills.

5. *Social treatment groups.* Preston-Shoot (1987) divides these into four types: (a) groups aiming to maintain or enhance existing adaptive behaviours; (b) groups aiming to modify behaviours which are not seen as helpful to the members; (c) problem-centred groups aiming to help members to resolve their own difficulties via group support; and (d) groups aiming to provide compensatory experiences for members who have been deprived of earlier experiences.

6. *Discussion groups.* These groups focus on matters of general interest to members rather than problem orientations.

7. *Self-help group.* These groups have a range of purposes. Their distinguishing characteristic is that the worker's role is either minimal or non-existent. Often the members organize the group themselves or the worker is available only for occasional advice or consultancy. There is further discussion of these groups in Chapter 4. See also Habermann (1990).

8. *Social action groups.* These groups utilize the members' collective power as a vehicle for campaigning for social change. Likely targets are road safety, welfare rights, housing standards, or protests to stop particular local developments such as open cast mining or development on ecologically sensitive sites (Sutton 1994).

9. *Self-directed groups.* Like self-help groups, the focus of these groups may have a range of purposes but their salient feature is their relationships with workers. Workers are present only to help members determine the direction of the group and achieve its aims. There is further discussion of these groups in Chapter 4. See also Mullender and Ward (1991).

Both Preston-Shoot (1987) and Douglas (1995) relate types and characteristics of groups to their purposes. Douglas states that the choice of principal characteristics selected are those most likely to serve the main purpose of the group. Preston-Shoot (1987) suggests that in selecting from the above classification, 'groupworkers will be influenced by the goals they have in mind, the style of work and leadership which they favour and the assumptions and value-base which underpin their practice' (p.17).

Group purposes are further explored in Chapter 4.

Discipline differences?

Is it helpful, indeed possible, to relate different types of groups to agency purpose or the professional disciplines of group workers? Such categorization might be based on the ideological context of the agency, the client group, the main theoretical framework used in a group or the groupwork educational approaches in the training of particular professions. This is a complex task and preliminary researches suggest that group workers across all professional backgrounds tend to be very eclectic. It may be useful, however, to explore whether we can discern the major influences on group workers and their agencies. Of particular interest would be whether there are any clear differences related to individual practitioner's professions or whether their agency ethos is a better predictor of conceptual framework.

The literature drawn on by group workers and on booklists of caring professionals' qualifying programmes falls broadly under three headings: psychiatry, social psychology and general groupwork.

Psychiatry

Dwivedi's (1993) book on groupwork for children and adolescents, while providing a broad range of references and ways of working, is firmly rooted in child psychiatry and the child and family consultation service. There is a long tradition of group psychotherapy for children and adults (Yalom 1975, 1985) emanating from psychiatric services and mental health agencies.

Psychiatric references are most likely to be found on lists of recommended books on nursing courses, rather than those of other caring professions. However, the degree to which groupwork is part of the nursing curriculum varies widely between different institutional programmes, as does the emphasis on particular groupwork approaches. There does, however, seem to be a tendency for mental health nursing routes to be more likely to provide groupwork as a core part of the curriculum than other nursing routes, as well as being more likely than other professions to include psychiatric texts on groupwork booklists. So while nursing booklists may well include social psychology and general groupwork texts, there remains a greater tendency to include psychiatric references than for the other caring professions.

These, however, are tendencies. The group run by a community mental health nurse in the examples given in Chapter 2 is clearly cognitive behavioural, while the Women's Group, which has a social worker leader, clearly has a psychodynamic base.

Social psychology

The degree to which programmes for caring professionals teach groupwork as core curriculum is very varied, but occupational therapists and youth workers generally view groupwork as a central professional tool. All caring professions' qualifying programmes that specifically teach groupwork rely on a broad range of social psychology references (Argyle 1981; Atkinson and Wells 2000; Borman 1990; Cooper 1986; Nelson-Jones 1986). Occupational therapists' groupwork booklists tend to represent the breadth of this profession, so that the list will include a basis of social psychology with some specific occupational therapy groupwork references (Cole 1999; Finlay 1993), probably some psychotherapy and a range of specific topics of relevance to this profession: art therapy, drama, dance, music, relaxation, anxiety management, massage and assertiveness.

General groupwork

All groupwork booklists across the caring professions are likely to draw on Benson 1987; Brown 1994; Douglas 1976, 1991, 1995; Johnson and Johnson 1987 and Preston-Shoot 1987. These texts are likely to be the core references for youth and community work programmes and social work students. Youth and community work texts also tend to list counselling references (Egan 1994; Rogers 1992), as well as specific professional ones (Harris 1994; Wheal 1998). Social work references may well include some psychotherapy and social psychology but will be predominantly general groupwork texts.

Many group workers are not easily categorized into a particular profession, and many other group workers were professionally trained some time ago so that they may not have had any groupwork focus on their qualifying programmes. In addition, group workers tend to select from the available literature those elements of interest to them, so that they evolve a particular perspective regardless of their professional base. Thus the above observations only represent some tendencies and do not account for the theoretical framework of particular workers.

Does agency ethos affect the groupwork focus?

Our small sample in Chapter 2 suggests not. The mental health setting and the substance misuse agency both have psychodynamic and behavioural groupwork, although the former is an NHS mental heath agency and the latter a mainly social work setting in the voluntary sector. Conversely, however, we would expect to find psychotherapeutic groups in a child or adult psychiatric setting.

It may be more pertinent to try to categorize groups according to the theoretical framework selected.

Theoretical frameworks

The purpose, and therefore type, of group, with its concomitant characteristics, will be selected through a complex set of interactive elements which include the worker's and the agency's value base, and the worker's preferred style and theoretical frameworks.

The descriptions of practice groups in Chapter 2 clearly illustrate how the choice of theoretical framework affects the whole ethos of the group, which includes all major characteristics, such as leadership styles, member selection imperatives, size, purpose, duration, programme and throughput. The interrelated nature of all these decision points, however, makes it difficult to ascertain which came first, the purpose or the theoretical perspective.

The Girls' Group and the Men's Group could both be seen as having a *sociological* theoretical base (see, for example, Giddens 1987). This perspective emphasizes the social structural elements which shape individuals' lives rather than the responsibility of the individual.

Groupwork using this approach is likely to have purposes such as empowering group members who are seen to be disempowered or stigmatized by the particular social structures of which they are a part. The group is likely to focus on power issues and provide strategies for improving members' social roles.

The aims of the Girls' Group were to: raise awareness of gender discrimination, and to empower these young women to recognize, challenge and combat gender discrimination via improved self-confidence (Langan and Day 1992). The ways in which the programme sought to achieve these aims is clearly related to its sociological conceptual framework. The purposes are achieved by a range of enjoyable activities which improve confidence and group mutual support but do not include any analysis of members' motivations or personal circumstances. Group membership is open and selection criteria only restricted to age and gender.

The main aim for the Men's Group, for men who are main carers of young children, was to provide a supportive forum for lone fathers. The workers felt that the social supports available to lone mothers do not seem to be so readily available to lone fathers.

Since the group's aim was to provide a supportive structure, the actual programme content did not seem of particular importance. It was, however, seen to be important that the members themselves contribute to the initiation of this content, as part of creating a supportive environment. In reality the group programme became deciding on group content over a number of weeks. Here again, group discussion did not focus on individual problems or solutions. Group membership was initially open but closed in later weeks, while membership was restricted to lone fathers.

The Women's Group could be seen as having a *psychodynamic* theoretical base (see, for example, Pearson, Treseder and Yelloly 1988). This perspective can take a variety of forms, but usually it includes an emphasis on feelings and self-disclosure and is based on the assumption that people's present motivations and behaviours are a response to complex past experiences, some of which are likely to be in early childhood. Groups with this theoretical base may focus on interpretations of members' behaviour in the group as a way of promoting members' insight into their own motivations. This method may include making assumptions that behaviour towards other members is a response to previous relationships and experiences in earlier life or present experiences outside the group.

The aim of the Women's Group is to provide a supportive environment with some treatment elements for women with substance and alcohol misuse issues. This programme content comes entirely from the members. Each member bids for time in which the group discusses issues of concern to them. The group members look for solutions to these issues and reinforce one another's attempts to grapple with helpful strategies. One of the treatment elements here is the use of Gestalt therapy. Since membership is open and constantly changing, much of the group time is spent inducting new members and ensuring that they continue the existing group processes.

The Positive Parenting Group has many elements of a *task-centred approach* (see, for example, Doel and Marsh 1992). This approach is a focused, time-limited framework offering problem-solving processes. It acknowledges that people with problems both need help with, and can contribute to, their problem sloving. It has a strong element of empowering users and of partnership between practitioners and users in a tandem approach to problem solving.

The Positive Parenting Group aims to support parents by promoting child–parent relationships via the improvement of parenting skills. The elements of this group which relates it to task-centred approaches are the centrality of members setting their individual goals, the involvement of members in keeping or rejecting particular group exercises, the continued relationship between selected exercises and members' individual goals and the use of individually tailored home tasks to be completed between meetings. In all these aspects users are seen as having a clear partnership role in setting, working towards and achieving their personal goals. The ethos of the group is a sharing environment in which workers will abandon prepared exercises if they no longer meet the needs of users.

This is a closed group with two leaders. The theoretical framework and a range of possible exercises have been used previously but workers are ready to adapt the overall parameters to meet members' needs.

The Anger Management Group, and to a lesser extent the Male Offenders' Group and the Anxiety Management Group, can be seen as having a *cognitive behavioural* theoretical base (see, for example, Wolpe 1982). This approach harnesses the psychological concepts of learning theory in order to offer a range of ways of changing behaviour and increasing the number of coping strategies available to the individual. Very specific goals are set by the client. These must relate to observable behaviours. The process usually begins with a behavioural assessment. This is to set a baseline around which antecedent behaviour can be established and specific gains in changed behaviour monitored. Monitoring is often done via home tasks. These may shape the desired behavioural goals over time, so that small improvements are reinforced with praise and the whole goal achieved by self-monitoring and gradual change. The cognitive elements of this approach consist of helping people understand why their behaviour manifests itself and in thinking about ways of dealing with it.

The Anger Management Group fits this approach very closely. It aims to help members understand how anger is manifested and dealt with by the individual, now and in the past. It has two behavioural goals: to help individuals identify areas of desired personal change, and to teach a range of behavioural techniques for the appropriate containment of anger.

The programme content consists of a number of exercises, many of them done individually, as well as general discussion and group exercises such as brainstorms. Many of the paper exercises are self-monitoring formats which members complete as homework tasks.

The Anxiety Management Group has an informational and educational approach in the first six weeks, but weeks 7 and 8 are devoted to teaching members the principles of self-behavioural management so that they can manage their personal issues in these terms after the group has ended. The Male Offenders' Group, although not purely cognitive behavioural, like the Anger Management Group, provides a number of self-monitoring exercises together with programme elements designed to change attitudes and responses.

Chapter 2

Groups in Practice

The following eight case studies illustrate the preparation and decision-making processes of a range of groups in their initial planning phases. These include groups in the voluntary and statutory sectors and represent a range of disciplines and client groups.

These agencies have co-operated with the author to provide detailed information about how and when initial group planning decisions were made. Relevant agency staff were interviewed with the same interview schedule which provided five areas on which to focus the discussion.

1. The Girls' Group (youth service, social worker and youth worker)

2. The Anxiety Management Group (community mental health team, occupational therapist and social work student)

3. The Men's Group for men who are main carers of young children (social services, two social workers)

4. The Male Offenders' Group (probation service, three probation officers)

5. The Positive Parenting Group (a national children's voluntary agency, two agency workers)

6. The Women's Group (voluntary agency for drug and alcohol misuse, social worker)

7. The Anger Management Group (voluntary agency for drug and alcohol misuse, agency worker)

8. The Women's Mental Health Group (mental health day hospital, community mental health nurse and an occupational therapist)

Succeeding chapters will draw heavily on these practice examples to explore the dilemmas facing practitioners in the initial groupwork phases.

The following provides a description of each group, as described by the group organizer, under each of the five headings. This chapter will not offer an analysis of any aspects of these groups but will only attempt to provide a case-study approach. This will be drawn on in succeeding chapters to illustrate theory and relate elements of decision making to outcome.

The Girls' Group

Group structure

The group was initially set up for young females aged 13 to 25 in a community centre run by the youth service. This is in a poor, central-city location. The centre already provided a number of youth groups, but the initiator, a social work student on a year 2 placement, felt that the boys tended to dominate these groups. She felt that since the boys were noisier and more demanding than the girls they tended to receive more staff attention. More resources also seemed to be spent on the boys since the equipment provided tended to be used almost exclusively by the boys: pool table, table tennis, football equipment. She felt that the girls were intimidated by the boys, the girls tending to have low self-esteem in this socially deprived area. There is also a 'red light district' nearby which the initiator felt provided a negative image for young females.

It was agreed by the agency that a group exclusively for young women should be set up to be jointly led by an experienced youth worker and the student initiator. The student had previously set up a group for Asian young women on her year 1 placement.

Meetings were to be held monthly since youth service funding could not provide more frequent meetings until the need was proven by demand.

The group began 18 months from the date of writing and continues to run. There were initially six members: two aged 17 years, one aged 15 years, one aged 14 years and two aged 13 years. After six months the starting age was lowered to 11 years and the meeting times changed from 7.30–9.30 to 7–9 p.m. A year after starting, the group had 11 members: one aged 14 years, five aged 15 years, three aged 11 years, two aged 17 years.

Group goals

The group goals were essentially the youth service goals for working with young women. However, at the first meeting the members were asked what they would like the group goals to be. All the members had ideas about boyfriends and brothers. They generally felt that boys got more attention than girls and that their mothers worked harder than their fathers. They expressed annoyance about this but felt resigned to its continuation. The two 17 year olds were A-level students and could therefore articulate these ideas into a set of objectives.

These are the aims and objectives which were printed on the introductory leaflet:

- Aims

  – to highlight the main issues and concerns young women face today

  – to offer one-to-one advice and support

  – to improve young women's awareness and understanding of sexual discrimination.

- Objectives

  – to empower young women to combat and challenge sexism and to recognise sexual discrimination

  – to provide equal opportunities for participation and choice

  – to enable girls and young women to develop to their full potential

  – to enable young women to develop their self-confidence and an understanding of their personal worth

– to enable girls and young women to 'have a go' at activities in a male-free and supportive atmosphere.

A year into the group the experienced youth worker was replaced by another experienced worker. The student had finished her placement but was offered seasonal work to continue working with the group. Since a new worker had arrived the two leaders decided to re-evaluate the objectives. This process was achieved with the group members and resulted in the objectives being translated into more user-friendly language; for example, equal opportunities, advice, support, awareness of discrimination, and self-confidence.

The leaders did not set formal goals for individual members but agreed that ongoing goals for individual members should be agreed and promoted between the leaders during the life of the group; for example, of two sisters, the older dominated the younger, so the leaders tried to encourage the younger one to contribute. Some young women needed help in improving their social skills and, in particular, social responses to others. The leaders used group processes to promote these responses.

Selection criteria

Members were self-selected, but information was provided to the youth clubs and after-school clubs already run at the centre, as well as providing leaflets and posters in the locality. Some personal approaches were made to potential members and this proved to be the most effective way of recruiting members.

Age and gender were clear selection criteria while race and intellectual ability were not. There was some disagreement between the centre manager and the group initiator about the minimum age. The manager wanted it set at 13 years since this is the youth service remit. The social work student wanted it set at 11 years since she felt the younger age would provide better opportunities to make a difference to the young women's lives.

Group programme

The group activities were chosen by the leaders in consultation with the members. They planned that within four sessions, one would be an outing, one a fun session and two informal education. However, the latter two categories became fairly indistinguishable in practice.

Outings were made to Zapattack, bowling, the cinema and The Body Shop for makeovers. The members seemed very cohesive and supportive to each other on these outings and they seemed to be a very relaxed group.

Evenings at the centre followed a range of activities. A drum session was held in which each member had their own drum to beat. Everyone made lots of noise. The leaders thought that the members felt confident, released and happy, and that this activity allowed them to dominate the environment. Collages were made individually from women's magazines to illustrate woman's projected images. A cooking evening focused on healthy eating.

The girls seemed to enjoy all activities equally. Some enjoyed making collages more than the outing since making collages was more personal and creative, they could work with other members and they had considerable staff attention.

The members continue to offer ideas for sessions but generally the pattern has remained the same.

Size, time and space

There was no restriction placed on the number of members to be recruited since several groups could be formed. The group is open to any resident in the area.

The group runs for two hours. This is standard for youth service groups, since staff are paid for three-hour sessions to allow for a two-hour group plus preparation and evaluation time. The leaders felt this to be appropriate but outings would clearly take longer.

The sessions were held at the centre since the whole building was available at this time and so all the equipment – table tennis, pool table, darts, table football, computers, musical and sports equipment – could be used exclusively by the group without having to compete with the boys. The leaders hope that the girls will continue to use the equipment in a mixed-group situation.

The Anxiety Management Group

Group Structure

This group is run frequently by occupational therapy staff at a city centre community mental health team. The groups are led by a groupwork-experienced occupational therapist with a co-worker. This could be an occupational therapist inexperienced in groupwork or a suitable social work student on placement in this multidisciplinary team.

The group has eight weekly sessions of two hours each. This group began with ten invited members. Seven of these ten attended various sessions with four members attending very regularly.

This type of group is typically run by this health trust by occupational therapists in mental health settings: in community teams, day hospitals and rehabilitation day hospitals. It is therefore a well-used model, adapted by particular staff but clearly part of the expected workload of an occupational therapist in a mental health environment in this locality. This team also organizes a number of other groups: Assertiveness, Anxiety Management, Defeat Depression, and Self-Esteem. These all consist of eight sessions, and are closed.

Group goals

The group had four formal aims:

1. Develop an increased awareness of the *causes* and *effects* of stress and anxiety.

2. Introduce group members to a range of therapeutic techniques which are known to have some value in reducing unpleasant anxiety symptoms.

3. Encourage participants to observe their own behaviour in order to make positive changes.

4. Encourage group members to consider existing problems they may have within a supportive group environment and to adopt positive coping strategies for dealing with these.

The leader thought that since this has been a well-used format over a long period of time, the aims were partly historical. The leader intends to educate the clients about their illness and to help them to control it: 'educate and empower'.

Goals for individuals are set with members in the final two weeks of the programme, when they are taught the principles of behavioural management. They are not expected to have a full knowledge of this therapeutic approach but to grasp sufficient of the principles to be able to manage some of their own behaviours.

Selection criteria

Members can self-refer or can be referred by colleagues. These are usually community psychiatric nurses or social workers. However, all clients have been screened before referral to occupational therapists. Screening here is particularly for active psychotic symptoms and substance misuse. Potential members are home visited by the leader first to assess whether anxiety is the main issue and whether the client is motivated to work on it. This occupational therapist uses a questionnaire to assess these. Age is not a selection issue except users must fall within the age range for service provision, 18–65 years.

The race and gender balance of the group is rarely an issue but if the group has a single male, female or black potential member, the user is asked if they want to be in this group or to join a later one.

The personality of a potential member or their likely group behaviour would be a consideration if they seemed likely to disrupt the group. It is felt that people with learning disabilities will not benefit from this group.

Group programme

The model for this group is well established but leaders deviate from it in terms of the materials used to teach the content, the order of providing the content and in response to members' questions.

The model is an eight-week, two-hour group in which all sessions begin with relaxation. This is group relaxation for all members with 30 minutes of various techniques: tension release, autogenics, visualization, music and commentary. Some of these use pre-recorded tapes. In sessions 1–6 members are taught about the causes and effects of anxiety and a range of positive approaches. These sessions last from one to one-and-a-quarter hours. In weeks 7 and 8 the principles of behavioural management techniques are taught, and members begin to look at their personal issues in these terms. The pace varies according to the group's needs and the amount of group interaction. The group's leader had local access to a range of teaching materials for occupational therapists. These came from a variety of sources: mental health professionals, psychology and psychiatry texts. They covered some of the following areas: signs and symptoms; physiology; panic attacks; challenging irrational thoughts; avoidance behaviour; and desensitization programmes. Since there are several handouts on the same topic, leaders choose the ones they find most helpful.

At the end of the group members do an evaluation. This is often the HAD questionnaire which is nationally recognized and will usually have been used as an outcome measure at the beginning of the group so that progress can be measured.

Size, time and space

Group size is seen to be important, so no more than 12 would be invited. Six to eight is seen to be ideal. There is usually a mixture of members drawn from long-term clients from the team and clients referred from other professionals. All groups are closed. The group is held in a room in the premises used by the community mental health team. In physical terms it is a pleasant room and is seen to be ideal for teaching, but it is too small for relaxation exercises. In terms of client identity, the leader feels that the community team rooms do not feel too stigmatized and are certainly better than hospital premises. However, the presence of a residential mental health unit attached to the team building, the leader feels, might make the venue stigmatized to some extent.

The Men's Group for men who are main carers of young children

Group structure

This group was initiated by two female social workers in a city-centre, generic social services team. One worker was an experienced child care worker with additional groupwork experience and the other an inexperienced worker. The group members were four men in their mid-twenties to forties. They were all lone carers of young children. Meetings were held weekly for one-and-a-half hours.

This was a pilot group initiated by the two workers in response to a need they had recognized as a result of having a number of lone male carers of young children on both their caseloads. The workers thought that the social supports used by lone mothers were not supportive to lone fathers and hoped the group would provide some support for them.

Group goal

The workers set the group goal, which was to provide a supportive forum for lone male carers of young children, so that they could support each other. They also had a covert goal for one of the members in that they hoped that one of the other members would influence his future choice of women.

Selection criteria

The only selection criteria was that members must be male and be lone carers of young children. Initially the members were drawn from the leaders' caseloads but when they had insufficient numbers, leaflets and posters were distributed. Members recruited by this process were therefore self-selected.

Group programme

Before the group began the leaders had had a number of ideas about the programme, speakers and some topics for discussion. Their ideas were only tentative, however, since they wanted the members to be involved in determining the group's activities. The selection of the programme in fact became a long process and stretched over five sessions. A detailed analysis of this process is recorded in Chapter 7. In reality, the sessions the group spent discussing appropriate activities became the core activities themselves.

Size, time and space

It was decided that the group should be open, but since members were likely to be sharing personal experiences it was expected that the group would become closed at a later date. In fact a new member joined the group on session 3. After this no new members joined, so the group was in actual fact closed.

The workers had thought that the group would meet monthly but the members wanted weekly sessions.

The group meeting room was considered with care by the workers. It was decided to hold it in a local family centre. This was a very comfortable room, furnished for adults and decorated with muted colours. It was felt to have a relaxing ethos. Two members of the group knew the centre. The leaders did not want to hold the group in social services premises and felt the family centre room was suitable for the purpose and would not have any negative connotations for the members.

Male Offenders' Group

Group structure

This group for male offenders was run within a probation service by two female and one male probation officers. It was a pilot group based on part of a group programme for offenders which had been used for some time in Northern Ireland.

The group had eight members aged 18 to 48 years. It ran for 18 weeks with sessions of two hours a week. The members were all designated as having low to medium risk.

All probation clients have pre-sentence reports. In this county they also have an ACE assessment. This was originally produced by another probation service and provides an 'offender group re-offending scale' score. This is a statistical probability score for each individual from factual data inputs. It defines the offender's level of risk. This provides information on the level of work needed and the degree of work intensity required.

The group was set up in response to changes in government policy on offenders in that probation services need to demonstrate their effectiveness in being tough on offenders. This probation service has a steering group for effective practice. It decided that this sector of the county should pilot a version of the Stop, Think and Change programme that had been used very successfully over a long period of time in Northern Ireland.

The offenders on this pilot will be monitored for re-offending rates.

Group goals

The leaders aimed to provide a group environment for members outside their daily pressures in which they could look at themselves and their offending behaviour in a supportive environment and talk about their issues with staff and other group members. They wanted to motivate members to feel that they could change their own lives. Another aim was to challenge racist and sexist attitudes.

In addition to aims for individual change for group members, the service also related this pilot group to institutional probation service changes. The steering group wanted to promote a service culture which provides more service-wide initiatives and less individual probation officer work with offenders.

The overall aims for the group are the same as for the Northern Ireland model with the exception of the latter.

There were no formal goals for individual group members but the leaders did have hopes for some members; for example, that one member would not drink alcohol during group meetings. Individual work could be undertaken if assessed as necessary by group leaders.

Selection criteria

The selection criteria was partly defined by the steering committee and partly by the leaders, in that some of the principles, such as levels of risk, were set by the steering committee but the leaders selected the actual members via existing pre-sentencing reports and the ACE assessments. In addition no sex offenders or very vulnerable clients were selected. The latter were felt to be unable to cope with the group. Members had to be male. Race, socio-economic group and age were felt to be irrelevant. Educational level was not relevant except that those with learning disabilities would not be able to complete some of the paperwork in some of the exercises. It was therefore expected that they would need sensitive additional support. Previous history, personality and likely group behaviour were all taken into account by the ACE assessment.

Group programme

The whole Stop, Think and Change programme, which was franchised from the Northern Ireland service, was written for high-risk offenders, each of the three topics being written in separate parts. This service decided to use only the Stop element and to adapt the programme for medium-risk clients. The leaders therefore selected only three of the Stop units: New Start, Men Talking and Facing Up to Offending.

NEW START

This mainly consisted of introductory processes: agreeing ground rules, brainstorming purposes of the group and icebreaker exercises. Later, members also discussed their previous learning experiences, the dynamics of the group, and did some role reversal role plays with clients playing probation officers.

MEN TALKING

The leaders felt this to be the most successful unit of the three.

By this stage the male leader was off sick and so this unit was led entirely by female staff. The exercises were provided by the programme but had to be considerably adapted. The female leaders did, in fact, use this unexpected circumstance to their advantage. The sessions were mainly group exercises followed by discussion. The group was asked to list gains and losses in their own experiences of the transition from boy to man. The leaders then asked what response they thought women would have to these male attitudes and expectations. Another exercise involved drawing masks to illustrate how their roles changed in different circumstances, particularly in relation to partners, work and leisure. The group also made some collections of images of men from magazine clips.

FACING UP TO OFFENDING

The focus of this unit was personal responsibility for offending behaviour. The method again consisted of paper exercises and discussion. In common with unit 2 the given exercises were adapted by the leaders to suit the clients' needs. They felt more able to do this in units 2 and 3 since confidence and group trust had now built up. In addition to looking at their own offending behaviour the members also discussed the experiences of their victims: 'What statements might your victims make about the effects of your offending behaviour?'

At the end of the programme each member evaluated their own progress and all felt that they had contemplated change in their lives and/or made some active changes.

Size, time and space

This was a closed group. The group began with eight members, although only five completed the programme. The leaders would have liked 12 but there were pressures to make a start.

The group was held in the probation day centre in the probation service building. It was a large, comfortable room with a pool table, and tea and coffee making facilities. The leaders felt it was a very relaxed environment and very appropriate for the purpose. They felt the venue to be very important. It was deliberately held on probation premises since they wanted the members to have a positive image of the service.

The Positive Parenting Group

Group structure

This group was run by a national children's voluntary agency in a family centre, with two leaders. It was a closed group with a flexible duration of 12 to 16 weeks. It was set up in response to requests from other agencies, such as the local school, who wanted parents to be helped to improve their parenting skills. Parents who already attended the family centre were also asking if the centre would run such a group.

Group goals

The two leaders saw the group as having two central goals – to:

1. promote child/parent relationships

2. support parents in identifying parenting skills in relation to child management issues.

All prospective members were invited to an introductory session. At this session parents were asked to think about their personal goals in relation to the purpose of the group. Parents were encouraged to set personal targets; for example, better awareness of developmental stages, to deal more effectively with temper tantrums.

All prospective members are visited at home after the introductory session to set individual goals. This process helped prospective members decide whether this group would be appropriate for them. There were no drop-outs from the introductory session.

Selection criteria

This group began with 12 members, of whom five were self-referrals and seven were referred by social services, health visitors, woman's refuge and the education department. After two weeks three of the agency referrals had dropped out. Two members from the woman's refuge had transport problems. A member referred by social services was felt by her social worker to need more in-depth one-to-one work than the group could offer.

Two of the prospective members had learning difficulties. This did not exclude them, but the leaders suggested to them that they would need some additional support. The personality or likely group behaviour of prospective members was not a consideration for group inclusion but would be dealt with in the group if it became a problem. If this was not helpful over time, then the leaders would work with the member in question outside the group. Gender balance would only be an issue in some circumstances. If there was only one male member he would be asked if he still wanted to be part of this group. If there were women in the group from the refuge who had experienced domestic violence it was unlikely they would be put in a group with a lone male member. If women in these circumstances expressed a concern about being in a group with men, then the workers would provide an all-women group.

The workers were not concerned that some members were self-referrals while others were agency referred. Concern would be felt if there were considerable differences in need between members.

In the past a group had been run for four women, all of whom had experienced domestic violence. This was because of the degree of problems being experienced as a result of domestic violence. The smaller group was able to provide more in-depth support. The parents had similar problems and so could be more supportive to each other. The workers had assumed that the children would have similar problems to each other, and this proved to be so.

Group programme

The group programme was decided by the leaders following the home visits, when individual goals were set. The leaders proposed a range of group methods all based on task-centred exercises. After each session the leaders and members reflected on the exercises so that sometimes activities were dropped or repeated.

The activities consisted of relaxation, role play, discussions, and small and large group exercises. An example of an exercise would be: think of a positive childhood experience, feed it back to the whole group. All exercises were tailored to the specific needs of the group members. Members were given home tasks between meetings.

Size, time and space

Group size was agreed to be between 8 and 12. This was partly for practical reasons and partly for theoretical reasons. At least eight parents was thought to be a good number to feel like an identifiable group and, it was hoped, provide a supportive group for each other. The leaders felt that the members would have a broad range of needs which would be difficult for one leader to manage alone. It is easier for the agency to justify using two leaders at one time if the group has at least eight members. The group was closed since the leaders felt that it takes time for members to trust each other and to share issues of personal concern to them. The leaders thought that new members change the dynamics of a group.

The sessions lasted for one to one-and-a-half hours. This was decided due to practical considerations relating to crèche facilities and collecting times for the parents of school-age children.

Duration was agreed to be between 12 and 16 weeks. Twelve weeks was thought to be the minimum in which the parents' needs could be met. It was also thought that more than 16 weeks creates a dependency on the leaders. Practice wisdom had clearly illustrated in the past that this type of group, given its objectives, needs this length of programme to plan, record, evaluate and respond to members' needs during the sessions.

The room used was a medium-sized dining-room in the centre. It was seen as a relaxing environment since it is used as a coffee-cum-social room for centre users. It was thought to be good for the purpose since it was sufficiently large for people to have private conversations and to sit out of the group. It therefore provided a level of personal choices.

The Women's Group and the Anger Management Group are run by the same voluntary agency. This is an agency for people with drug and alcohol misuse problems. It provides both residential and day care services in a city centre. The two groups have workers from different disciplines and are based on very different theoretical perspectives. They are also the only groups in the case studies that have single worker/organizers.

The Women's Group

Group structure

This group has been running for ten years. It is an open group and has an average of ten members aged 24 to 55. This is typical of the agency population. There are more day clients than residents, usually one resident to two day clients, but the residential population is only about 8 to 12 people. Meetings are weekly for two hours. The group has a single facilitator. This is partly for historical agency reasons but also because the agency feels this type of group needs only one worker to identify key needs and check resources. This worker is a qualified social worker with a practice teacher's qualification to allow her to take students on placement in her agency.

Group goals

Initially the group was set up to provide a separate space for women to raise issues of importance to them around alcohol misuse. At this time there were a number of women with alcohol misuse issues only. The group is now concerned with both alcohol and drug misuse as most clients have issues around both. This is primarily a support group with counselling and therapy functions and some Gestalt elements. The support-plus-therapy-style group is central to this agency's ethos; the Gestalt elements, while shared with a number of colleagues, are part of the professional style of the present worker. This worker is the third worker with this group.

Selection criteria

All potential members are assessed at a prior meeting to discern whether this group is likely to be helpful for them. The main reasons why joining this group could be seen as unhelpful are that it would not be the right time for the client to join the group because they need to work more slowly, but they may join later, or, less likely, that they have a history of disruptive behaviour in groups. Clearly all members are women. Each new member has an initial four-week period in the group to assess whether it suits them.

Group programme

Initially the programme content came entirely from contributions from the members. After around three years there seemed to be few contributions from members so it was decided to provide a structure of topics with some outside speakers. The original structure is now in place: members raise issues at the beginning and bid for time in the group. The amount of time for discussion per topic is rationed by the worker and depends on how many people have bid for time. In the three months that the present worker has facilitated the group, there have always been plenty of bidders for time. The worker's role includes ensuring that quieter new members are included in general discussion and are not cut out by vociferous established members. Part of group session time is also taken up by the procedure for inducting new members. The new member is introduced by the worker, then each existing member says their name and makes one statement on how the group works. There is a lot of owning of the group by the members. This process reinforces group identity and agreed group goals and procedures. The group programme was originally decided by staff but the changes were jointly agreed by the members and the facilitator.

Size, time and space

The size of this group has naturally settled at around ten members so there has been no need to make decisions about upper limits. However, the worker feels that the structure would have to change if there were more than 15 members since it would be difficult to introduce new members and a second facilitator would be needed.

This group is open because it means that a group experience can be offered to new clients fairly immediately. The lack of structure also facilitates this. Because motivation to change substance misuse behaviour is usually low, the agency needs to offer around three open groups to new clients on arrival, thus grasping opportunities as quickly as possible. Its openness does, however, present some issues for the group. The group deals with difficult issues such as rape. The existing group members and facilitator have evolved ways of dealing with such issues which can be very daunting for new members. Old members also may not want to revisit subject matter that has been thoroughly discussed already, although new members want to raise it.

The group lasts two hours. It was previously one-and-a-half hours but was invariably short of time. The group has no break, no smoking is allowed and there are no tea or coffee breaks. This has been decided by the group members.

The group is held in a large room separated from the rest of the building. This implies that the group is formal, but it is a warm, carpeted room with easy chairs, providing a lot of personal space. The facilitator encourages members to move within the large space if they are unhappy with their position.

The Anger Management Group

Group structure

This is a pilot group designed as one of the agency's cognitive behavioural groups, which all clients attend. The groups each last six weeks, with each meeting lasting one-and-a-half hours. Clients usually attend three a week so that in six months they will have attended all the agency's cognitive behavioural groups. Some are permanently provided and are part of a continuous programme, others are added, evaluated, adapted, and retained or dropped. All members of this group must have already attended the Stress Management Group, where they will already have learnt some skills and coping strategies, such as preliminary skills for containment of anger, relaxation techniques, and understanding triggers to angry behaviour. The group worker has an educational background in health sciences and has previously worked as a counsellor in the health services.

Group goals

The group has three overall goals and also goals for each session. The goals were devised by the worker but each member sets personal goals. Overall goals are to:

1. utilize a cognitive behavioural approach to understand how anger is manifest and dealt with in the individual's life, at present and in the past

2. enable members to identify areas of desired personal change

3. teach a selection of management techniques for containing anger appropriately.

The third goal will be altered in future groups. The worker had expected members to exhibit explosive behaviour, but several members dealt with their anger inwardly, which led to self-harming behaviour such as self-burning and cutting, rather than explosive behaviour.

The goals for each of the six-week sessions were:

1. how to understand and recognize anger: personal triggers

2. triggers analysed: chains of events, analysis of actual past events

3. consequences of angry behaviour: existing skills, personal targets for change

4. alcohol and anger information: positive self-statements as a control technique

5. learning to reduce tension using assertiveness skills: when to express anger

6. reframing, the ABC of anger control, receiving anger, ending and evaluation.

Selection criteria

The eight pilot group members were aged between 22 and 50, half of them male and half female, and all white. This is typical of the agency's client group. All members needed to indicate that they had anger management issues. They must be able to interact in a group and possess sufficient understanding and energy to gain from the group experience. The worker would not have run a single-gender group but this is in any case unlikely to occur in this agency. Groups have in the past included single ethnic members and this has not been seen as problematic. The high level of paper exercises involved means that poor literacy would have been a problem.

Group programme

Each session, using the week's goal as a topic base, followed a structure of: brainstorm, use of new and homework handouts, and general discussion. Each session used some homework tasks to do exploration work in small groups, followed by a plenary summary of core points.

The programme is centred on the use of a large number of paper exercises, some to be kept by the members throughout attendance at the group, others as homework for particular sessions.

Some examples of the paper exercises include:

- an anger diary – a self-monitoring format to be kept as a homework task throughout the group
- an objectives checklist – personal targets for which a format was provided with suggested content but space for additions. Reference was made to these personal objectives as different strategies were tried during the group
- an anger breakdown form – a format to track single incidents of anger (very successful)
- limits of your self-control – a very useful monitoring format for some, confusing for others
- self-monitoring format – members were supposed to tick a box when a personal target was achieved. However, the list of provided achievements was too similar to the objectives checklist and there was confusion between the lists.

Many of these exercises have now been revised in light of the experience of the pilot group. The exercises were drawn from some clinical psychologist's examples, and general reading.

Size, time and space

It was agreed the group size should no more than ten and no less than five. This is agency practice wisdom for a group of this type. The group was closed after week 2, since shared personal experiences need the security of a given group of people. The group lasted one-and-a-half hours, which is the norm in this agency for this type of behavioural group. This is partly due to staffing resources. The meetings were held in the group room, which is seen as comfortable and separate from the rest of the agency.

The Women's Mental Health Group

Group structure

This group is run by a community mental health nurse and an occupational therapist, in a healthcare trust, mental health day hospital. It has been run in its present form three times over the last year. It was previously organized with another occupational therapist in a different format. This day hospital also runs an assertiveness group, an anxiety management group and a depression group. These are all led by occupational therapists with a mental health nurse co-working.

The group meets weekly, for one-and-a-quarter hours, for six weeks. The groups may begin with about nine members but often settle down to about five or six members. All clients are referred by other agencies and are assessed by an allocated key worker on arrival at the day hospital. Individual women's likely needs to join this group are often recognized at this initial assessment, so that there is usually a waiting list for the next group. However, members can join later if they are still attending the day hospital, via a referral from their key worker.

This day hospital had previously run an activity-based health issues group for women. Each week a particular issue would form the focus of the meeting. However, this community mental health nurse felt that women at the day hospital needed the chance to offer each other mutual support and to focus on women's issues around their nurturing roles. The occupational therapist had similar ideas.

Group goals

The group aims to offer women the opportunity to consider how women's day-to-day lives affect their health and, via mutual support, to find positive ways of improving psychological and physical well-being. The group's focus is on life situations of particular importance to women, and is concerned chiefly with current, rather than past, issues. The core concern of the group workers is to help the members increase their insight into how aspects of their daily lives impact on their mental health, and to encourage them to take charge of their own lives to restore the balance. The group promotes the idea of self-indulgence and uses the injunction 'be selfish' to challenge women's traditional view of what being selfish may mean. The group logo is a jug. This symbolizes that women need to replenish their own self-nurturing supplies. The group workers' viewpoint is that many women nurture their families, their jobs and their social networks, but give insufficient attention to their own nurturing needs. These goals were defined by the workers, but goals are not set for individual members and mutual support is a strong element of the group processes.

Selection criteria

Gender is a clear selection criteria in this group but age, ethnicity and sexuality are not. Potential members are initially assessed and information from outside sources is also taken into account. Clients with particular diagnoses will not be excluded but those with personality disorders or psychoses could be excluded if they are seen to be insufficiently stable and likely to affect other group members. Since most potential members are on a waiting list, key workers are consulted before a new group begins to ascertain whether the client is still attending the day hospital and whether this group continues to fit the user's needs.

Group programme

This group has a very well structured programme, which mainly consists of a number of exercises, completed by individuals in small-group situations. Members also have homework tasks to do between sessions. The workers do not see the group as having a specific theoretical approach but view it as mainly client centred with some cognitive behavioural elements. The exercises are generally fairly self-explanatory worksheets. The workers try to encourage members to complete the sheets without the workers' commenting on how the members are progressing. The sheets are completed in small groups which do not include the workers. The small groups then feed back to the large group and a general discussion is then based on the small-group work. Each of the six sessions has a specific topic.

Session 1
Aims and rules of the group
Introductory exercises
Introduction of the 'jug' concept

Session 2
Homework feedback
Positive and negative aspects of life stages
Introduction of the 'be selfish' concept
Homework

Session 3
Homework feedback
Life roles, positives and negatives
Changes to make to life roles
Homework

Session 4
Homework feedback
Vicious circles
Breaking out of vicious circles
Homework on 'being selfish'

Session 5
Homework feedback
Circle of repetition
Homework

Session 6
Homework feedback
Tree of opportunity symbol

Return to jug concept
Group evaluation.

During these sessions a number of painful issues are explored by members, who support each other. Many of these women are socially isolated. The group is intended as a supportive friend or neighbour. Both members and the workers reassure and make suggestions about strategies. The focus is on positive roles and the reduction of negative effects. Homework encourages members to take 'selfish' action at home in order to enhance positive aspects of their lives and thereby improve their mental health.

Size, time and space

This is a closed group since it is felt that the group processes require continuity and a build-up of trust between members. The maximum number of members would be 12 and the minimum three. A weekly meeting is seen to be helpful since it enables the homework tasks to become embedded in members' daily lives.

Meetings are held in the clients' non-smoking lounge. This is large enough for small groupwork and is reasonably comfortable. It is felt to be fairly homely but it could be a more comfortable environment.

Chapter 3

Power, Race and Gender

Empowerment

Power issues, together with all aspects of anti-discriminatory practice, are clearly fundamental issues for any professional to consider throughout the processes of group work. They are particularly so in the planning phases of a group. Although all aspects of anti-discriminatory practice will affect the processes and outcomes of a group, space here will only permit an examination of some race and gender issues to be considered in initial group planning.

The whole process of group work is concerned with the power relationships between group members, and leaders and members. An examination of these power relationships is a neglected area of group-work literature and is often disguised as group dynamics, of which of course it is certainly a part. In human services literature in general, there has been a recent growth in the examination of power relations. There is also a growth in texts which are specifically about empowerment. Much of this discussion has useful insights for groupwork. Braye and Preston-Shoot (1995, p.3) set out to 'encourage workers to negotiate the power dynamics of their relationships with users, to develop skills in working within the ethos of empowerment and partnership'. They explore the complexities of empowering service users in social care practice.

To a great extent empowerment is an overworked, often ill-defined, concept within a range of caring professions. However, at best it represents the complexity of interactions between the value systems held by the various professions and the broad range of anti-discriminatory practice. It is perhaps due to this complexity, and because the concept is used in such a variety of contexts, that it has tended to be overworked and underdefined. It does nevertheless represent an ideal set of dynamics and value positions in the relationships between service users and caring professionals. As such it is the basic premise for groupwork in the caring professions. In addition to providing a general value base for member–leader relations, it is also used to describe one of the main goals of any group.

In Chapter 2 the Anxiety Management Group has its defining aim as 'educate and empower'. The Girls' Group's main goal is to improve members' self-esteem and confidence. The Positive Parenting Group and the Men's Group for men who are main carers of young children aim to enable parents to feel more confident in taking control of their lives, particularly in relation to parenting. In turn, the Male Offenders' Group wanted to empower members to re-examine their offending behaviour and make new life choices. The Women's Group's focus is on empowering women to change their substance misuse behaviour, while the Anger Management Group aims to help members achieve their desired personal changes. The Women's Mental Health Group is centred on helping women to raise their self-esteem so that they can replenish their own self-nurturing abilities by redefining their own social roles rather than accepting the societally imposed role of nurturing others. Social care groups are organized to bring about change for users by enabling them to bring about change in their own lives or perceptions, or by enabling the group to act on their local or national environment to bring about structural change in the society. Many groups are initiated to ameliorate the perpetuation of continuing social inequalities.

This conceptual framework, in terms of values and ideologies related to user–worker relationships, is useful for professionals with acknowledged power who are trying to use their professional skills as leaders to empower group members.

Power, leaders and members

Many elements of the power relationships between members and leaders are established at the initial conception of the group. This relates to the type of groupwork planned and, more specifically, the way the leadership role is envisaged. Habermann (1990) draws distinctions between the roles of professionals working with self-help groups rather than social group work, although she acknowledges that the aims are often the same: to raise consciousness and mobilize resources. However, in practice differences in professional roles are not very distinct between a professional worker supporting self-help groups and the role of leader/worker in some supportive groups. In essence Habermann (1990) sees the main difference between these two types of groups in the fact that self-help members themselves set the agenda, set limits, and determine the tempo and organization of the group.

Habermann (1990) has a useful typology to describe the different roles a professional worker plays with self-help groups:

- Initiator
- Facilitator
- Consultant.

These roles only relate to professional workers in relation to self-help groups.

The Initiator role describes a situation in which the professional worker initially sets up the group by becoming aware of a need, invites potential members and helps the group to formulate its goals. The worker would then, after perhaps two meetings, leave the group to continue on its own as a self-help group.

The Facilitator role focuses on helping a self-help group to establish itself. This role particularly involves providing practical help such as a meeting room or publicity materials.

In the Consultant role the worker makes her professional knowledge available to the group without dominating it; that is, by providing professional insights only when necessary and ensuring the group remains a self-help one. Habermann (1990) acknowledges the difficulty of treading this fine line and provides some helpful discussion on the issues involved.

Mullender and Ward (1991) provide another dimension in the power position between group members and professional worker roles, with their concept of 'facilitator rather than leader of the group'. This concept should not be confused with Habermann's (1990) concept of Facilitator. The essence of this process of facilitation is one of enabling members to articulate their own goals and actions to achieve these. Facilitators must ensure that they are not directive, so that the users take responsibility for their own decisions and events. The role, however, is not one of non-intervention. It is an active role but not a dominant one. This role includes many of the group worker's familiar skills, such as helping communication, listening actively, encouraging participation and energizing. All this is central to the Facilitator's role as long as the members have set their own goals and they are not in fact the worker's goals. The worker's role in these 'maintenance' functions will, however, reduce as the members take on more responsibilities for maintaining the group. The Facilitator will also challenge sexism and racism as they arise in group meetings, since they are contrary to the worker's practice values.

In time the worker's role may recede, so that the worker becomes a consultant to the group. The group may become a self-directed group. The members have been empowered, in that the knowledge and skills have passed increasingly over time from the group workers to the group members.

In contrast to Mullender and Ward (1991) and Habermann (1990), Johnson and Johnson (1987), having provided a comprehensive summary of concepts of leadership in the literature, introduce an alternative perspective. Johnson and Johnson see all members of a group, including professional workers, as having leadership functions within the group. They define leadership as having two elements, Maintenance and Task functions. Maintenance is concerned with group members' behaviour which encourages the continuation of effective group functioning. Task is concerned with group members' behaviour which encourages the completion of the group's agreed tasks or goals. These two concepts are well interwoven in groupwork literature but not in the sense of the potentiality of attaching these skills to all members of the group. Clearly, in groups which have professional leaders, those leaders are expected to display both maintenance and task function skills. Johnson and Johnson are not discounting this but pointing out that members are likely to possess these skills as well. This is not in fact contrary to Mullender and Ward's (1991) views, but Johnson and Johnson see Task functions moving from skilled workers to group members via the self-directed empowerment process. This debate illustrates the complexity of power relations between members and group leaders across a range of groups from self-help to formal groups organized and managed by their leaders.

The above discussion focuses on the way that concepts of leadership may influence power relationships between workers and group members; but might another contributory factor be the function of the group itself?

Is it likely that power relationships will tend to be more formal in groups organized to change members' behaviour than in those organized to provide support for members? Certainly our case study groups illustrate that leaders who initiate a group in order to bring about some change in behaviour or attitude of their members are more likely to organize closed groups with specific durations. The programme is likely to be well defined, and planned and agreed between the leaders before the start of the group. This is well illustrated by the Male Offenders' Group, the Women's Mental Health Group and the Anxiety Management Group. All these groups had a format which had been used by previous groups. The groups have a well-defined, leader-decided programme. They are closed and of a specific duration.

The Girls' Group does not fit this model so well, since although it, too, is planned to change members' attitudes and the programme was largely chosen by the leaders, the membership remains open and the duration is continuing.

Groups set up to provide support for members are less likely to have these characteristics: the Men's Group for men who are main carers of young children initially remained open, the duration was not initially agreed and the programme evolved over a number of sessions. The power relationships between members here was very different. The social services workers may have initiated the group but the members were certainly enabled to set their own goals and activities at their own pace. The Women's Group is also an open group. Members bid individually to own part of each week's agenda, which is clearly not set by the worker. Interestingly, although the group's goal is to change attitudes to substance misuse behaviour, the worker describes this as a support group.

Power and race issues

As Brown (1994) states, small groups are a microcosm of the wider society: status and stereotypes will be transferred from the wider society to the group, reflecting the prejudice and structural inequalities of the society. Brown warns us that 'if they are not urgently and actively addressed and counteracted in the group, they will be perpetuated and reinforced' (p.155). Dominelli (1997, p.16) warns us that 'we will make mistakes because white supremacy has become such an integral part of our personalities and societal structures'. However, we are encouraged to continue striving: '...making mistakes and learning from them is preferable to taking no action at all'.

Power relations between members as well as those between leaders and members will clearly relate to anti-discriminatory practice dimensions as well as the broad range of group dynamics. It is beyond the scope of this book to include the latter which have been analysed by many group writers, such as Brown (1994), Douglas (1995) and Preston-Shoot (1987). However, we need to re-examine our familiar group dynamic perspectives of group processes in order to ensure that they are not obscuring processes of stereotyping and prejudice. Here we will consider only the areas of greatest concern to those engaged in planning groups in relation to race and gender issues.

Race

The two areas of greatest concern to professionals planning a group in relation to race are group composition and ethnic background of leaders. Workers planning groups clearly need to consider issues around race in relation to group composition. Choices about composition are not always in the hands of the leader. Open groups are in this category. Leaders often have pragmatic reasons for their group composition and clearly ethnicity issues are one of a number of considerations.

There seems to general agreement in the literature that workers should take care not to have a group with a very small number of members from any ethnic group. These members are likely not to identify with the group and its purposes, and to feel that their issues are being marginalized by the group members as a whole. Davis and Proctor (1989) point out that 'neither whites nor minorities appear to like being outnumbered' (p.115).

Group purpose will also affect whether race is a central criteria. If a group's goal is to raise consciousness, enhance the ethnic identity of a particular racial group, or to consider social action, then clearly it is appropriate to select members from that group.

The young people's group in Sheffield discussed by Mullender and Ward (1991) and the case study group for male offenders both have as stated goals the challenging of negative racial attitudes. Thompson (1997) warns that racist jokes are a vehicle for reinforcing and legitimating notions of racial superiority. Workers in these types of groups will need to challenge racist humour particularly, because it is perceived as not racist because it is humour. These are apparently mixed racial groups. Interestingly, this objective does not seem to influence their group composition decisions. The Sheffield group is open, and the Male Offenders' Group felt race, among some other possible criteria, to be irrelevant.

Did any of the case study groups consider race, in relation to group composition?

THE GIRLS' GROUP

The selection criteria of most concern to the group planners was gender and age. This fits with the group's goals since the main purpose was to raise the consciousness and self-esteem of young women. Apparently race and intellectual ability were not issues to be considered in the group's composition. Of the six initial members, one was Asian but no comment was made on this.

THE ANXIETY MANAGEMENT GROUP

The race balance of this group was an issue considered by the group leader. This balance was rarely an issue but if the group has a single black potential member, the user is asked if they want to join this group or join a later one.

THE MEN'S GROUP FOR MEN WHO ARE MAIN CARERS OF YOUNG CHILDREN

Race was not a selection criteria here. The only criteria was that members should be the main carers of young children.

THE MALE OFFENDERS' GROUP

Race, age and socio-economic group were felt to be irrelevant selection criteria here.

THE POSITIVE PARENTING GROUP

This group was mainly concerned with the group's gender balance. However, a single black potential member would be asked if they wanted to be in this group or join the next group. This is approached in the same way as the Anxiety Management Group. These groups are both run frequently by their agencies so that alternatives could be offered.

Race is not one of the main selection criteria for any of these groups. For some it was irrelevant because other criteria were more vital to their purposes. Others were concerned about racial balance in the sense that they wanted to reduce the likelihood of members feeling marginalized.

Davis and Proctor (1989) provide a comprehensive summary of research in the area of ethnicity and groupwork. This is mainly from the USA from the 1960s and 1970s. However, this may well provide useful insight for group workers in multicultural UK today. This research considers more complex questions than the possible marginalization of ethnic minorities in largely white groups. Davis and Proctor (1989) examine some of the issues around language and culture. They suggest that the first language of members is important. They also address cultural issues that exist within racial groups. This is of particular importance where group workers may assume that all Asian group members have the same language, culture and religion. These differences, they suggest, may influence member interactions significantly. This research also examines the relationship between racial composition and group dynamics. They found that members may be uncomfortable in groups of unfamiliar racial compositions, whether they are in the minority or not. It is thought that same-race members tend to provide more honest feedback They also surmised that cultural factors are likely to influence the content and direction of communication. It seemed that racially heterogeneous groups are better at 'enhancing positive interracial attitudes than groups...of all same race members' (p.116).

Ethnicity and co-working

Issues around the ethnicity of workers in groupwork, particularly in the UK, have almost no mention in the literature. This is a reflection of the general lack of references to ethnicity in groupwork literature in general. Exceptions to this are Brown (1994) and, more significantly, Mistry and Brown (1991). Mistry and Brown provide a comprehensive discussion of the broad range of issues around decisions about the ethnicity of workers in particular circumstances. This writing focuses on the 'dilemmas, principles and issues' (p.105) which may arise in black/white co-working contexts. The authors write from their personal experience as black and white co-workers in groupwork. They suggest that a black and white co-worker pairing is usually desirable in a racially mixed group, providing potential benefits for members. The desirability of this pairing, the authors suggest, varies considerably with the focus of group goals and the degree of formality of groups. In order to examine these dimensions four types of groups are discussed.

The first two are groups with the central goals of anti-racism. Here, one group has an all-white membership with black and white co-workers and the other has two black workers in an all-black members group. A number of issues for the workers are highlighted in each group. In the all-white members group some of the most salient issues were that the black worker was likely to have a higher status than the white worker and be expected to have expert knowledge; the black worker could become an object of anger if the members' attitudes are challenged; and the group is likely to test out the positive co-working relationship of the workers. In the all-black members group the two black workers were likely to be held in very high esteem; similar ethnic background members were likely to form an affinity to that worker; and the group was likely to produce a more satisfying experience for members than the all-white group.

The second two groups differ in their formality of structure. The first is a group for foster parents with black and white co-workers. Here it is likely that it will be the black worker who raises issues about the needs of black children or the stereotyping of black males. This has the potential to marginalize race issues and to imply that this worker is only interested in black issues. There also tend to be differences of opinion between these co-workers about whether racism ought always to be challenged and, if so, how. The second group is a racially mixed, offending behaviour group, in a probation service setting. This formal group style encouraged the workers to share the co-working task more equally. It may discourage dealing with race issues as they arise because of the formality of the pre-set format.

This, however, is not borne out by the first case study group. Frustration can also be caused to black members and co-workers if issues around racism in the criminal justice system as a whole are excluded from discussion.

Further comments by Brown (1994) and Mistry and Brown (1991) on the complexity of black and white co-working with mixed-race groups when a range of oppressions, including race and gender, arise accord with

Davis and Proctor's (1989) observations. Mistry and Brown (1991) also provide some very helpful frameworks for practitioners.

Power and gender issues

In many senses issues around gender and group composition are viewed in the literature (Brown 1994) as having similar principles as those of ethnic composition. Where member composition can be controlled, it is seen to be preferable not to have a gender minority. The degree to which this is a salient issue varies with the group's main objectives.

Gender seems to have been a considered issue in several of the case study groups. The Girls' Group was set up with its central objective being to change the young women's attitudes to themselves, and their relationship to the society and to young men in particular. Clearly gender and age were vital ingredients of group composition, and this requirement made it more difficult to recruit members in an environment where age is usually the only criteria.

The Men's Group for men who are main carers of young children also had a single-gender composition requirement. It too had some difficulties in recruitment since it also required members to be carers of young children.

The Male Offenders' Group, in its probation setting, given the dominance of male clients, had no difficulty in recruitment but, as with the Men's Group, there were gender issues around the leadership.

The Positive Parenting and the Anxiety Management Groups were concerned not to have a lone gender member but both left this decision to the users. This Positive Parenting Group had an all-female membership but, as Brown (1994) warns, inviting parents means the group is likely to include a minority of men who may well feel their needs are not being met and may well leave after a few sessions.

Five of the case study groups are specifically single-gender. The growth of single-gender groups can be traced through the women's movements of the 1960s and 1970s. These early groups were mostly developed to study women's issues and to provide a base for social action. They were not developed by the caring professions but were part of the broad women's movement. Alongside, and perhaps as a consequence of them, men's groups developed. These tended to have two kinds of objectives: either to encourage men to express their feelings and reflect more on affective aspects of their lives, or to deal with their violence and aggression. The Male Offenders' Group is clearly in the second tradition, while the Men's Group for men who are main carers of young children is mainly to support men who find themselves unsupported by a society which still regards child rearing as a female role.

The literature provides many examples of the growth of women-centred groupwork. Butler and Wintram (1991) provide a comprehensive approach to feminist groupwork. This book also includes an excellent feminist bibliography. Donnelly (1986), a student on a social work placement, worked in a voluntary agency on a socially disadvantaged city-centre estate. She set up a group for estate women to provide an empowering experience which focused on a feminist approach to power, poverty and gender issues.

The Girls' Group is in this tradition, since the members are drawn from a poor inner-city area, they have a low self-image and see their life chances as inferior to those of their contemporary male peers. Feminist issues are also clearly the ideological base for the Women's Mental Health Group with its mission to change the members' attitudes to their social roles. The Women's Group is firmly in the feminist tradition since its concern is to provide a space for women to look at their substance misuse behaviour.

Gender and co-working

Although issues around the worker's role in the group, and the particular considerations of co-working, are given considerable space in most groupwork references, such as Benson (1987), Douglas (1995) and Vernelle (1994), gender and co-working receive very little attention. However, Brown (1994) and Preston-Shoot (1987) provide some useful commentary. Preston-Shoot states that a male/female team may provide an effective model of male/female relationships for the group, although the purposes and composition of the group, as well as the co-workers' views, are all considerations. Brown (1994) says that if the group is all the same gender there needs to be a very good reason for not having at least one co-worker of the same gender. A central issue for such a lone worker, he suggests, would be the degree of gender stereotyping likely to be put on this worker. In a mixed-gender group, Brown suggests there should be at least one co-worker with whom members who are discriminated against can identify.

Co-working gender became an issue for both the Male Offenders' Group and the Men's Group for men who are the main carers of young children. The Male Offenders Group had intended to have mixed co-working with two female workers and one male worker. When the male colleague went sick after the first unit, the all-female workers had to adapt the unit's materials. Subsequently they used a specifically female perspective to elicit the members' viewpoints. This proved a very useful approach and this unit was the most successful of the three. However, this is not the same as beginning the group with all-female workers. By the time the male worker went sick the group had presumably settled and some trust had been built between workers and members. The Men's Group for men who are main carers of young children had two female workers from the start. They do not seem to have foreseen that this might be problematic. Initially there did not seem to be an issue here, but the workers experienced considerable hostility in session when the members began to talk about their negative experiences with women and to identify the female workers with women as a whole. This produced a very aggressive session with the members deliberately discounting the workers' ideas about group content.

The Girls' Group had two female workers. This seemed to work very well. One leader was later replaced by another female worker. The Positive Parenting and the Anxiety Management Groups both had female co-workers. Neither of these workers raised gender of co-workers as an issue although the former perhaps ought to have considered a positive male role model for this group. The Women's Group and the Anger Management Group both had single woman leaders. This decision was entirely due to agency policy but neither of the workers felt that this was inappropriate. It is very unlikely, however, that they would have accepted a male lone leader. The Women's Mental Health Group had female joint leaders and this was felt to be appropriate.

Chapter 4

Group Goals

The clarified goals of a group are the fulcrum on which meaningful decisions can be made about such preparation processes as: selection criteria, type of group activities, style of leadership, group size, frequency of meetings, and the premises required. There is considerable agreement in the literature (Brown 1994; Douglas 1995) that overarching group goals are the emergent product of the aims of the organization in which the group is set, and workers' goals and individual goals of members. It therefore seems likely that there is considerable variety in the extent to which there is clarity and consensus about group purposes among all the participants, and that there are a variety of ways in which groups reach agreement over overall group goals.

Preston-Shoot (1987) suggests that there are four categories of group goals: preventative, achieving external change, group centred and individual centred.

Preventative

This type of group provides support for people with similar needs or interests. They are likely to be isolated in the sense of having little contact with people with similar needs. The group provides 'a sense of belonging and mutual identity can lead to a change in social relationships and to members being able to...tackle...problems using the support, knowledge, ideas and experience acquired in the group' (Preston-Shoot 1987, p.19). Parents of children with particular disabilities and people recently experiencing a stroke would fit this category. The Men's Group for men who are main carers of young children was initiated to provide support and to prevent social isolation.

Achieving external change

These groups encourage social action in the community. They aim to challenge assumptions about power and who can act to achieve change. Users' rights are redefined and the group's focus is on the improvement in the quality of users' lives. Such groups are often structured as a multi-agency approach. Examples would be: community action to reduce local youth offending, wheelchair access to local shops and community action to improve housing resources.

Group centred

Here group goals are derived from the needs of the members. 'The group is used as a therapeutic resource, that is the resources of group members and group workers are used to achieve the group's objectives' (Preston-Shoot 1987 p.21). This category would be well illustrated by some types of self-help groups but perhaps relates more clearly to styles of worker roles than purposes of the group.

Individual centred

The focus here is on individual development and change. Objectives may be: the achievement of insight; understanding personal motivation and that of others; improvement of self-esteem; and the capacity to relate to others. This model fits well a wide variety of groups set up by caring profession workers. The Anxiety Management Group, the Male Offenders' Group and the Positive Parenting Group all fit this model.

The emergence of group goals

Although there is some agreement that group goals are the product of agency policy, practitioner interests and individual members' needs, there is less consensus about the process by which the group goals emerge. Johnson and Johnson (1987) define group goals as: 'A future state of affairs desired by enough members of a group to motivate the group to work towards its achievement' (p.133). In Johnson and Johnson's view some degree of consensus about group goals is a prerequisite for the group to exist, and certainly to continue to exist.

Earlier writers also viewed the group's main purpose as emerging from agency, workers' and users' goals. Hartford (1972) notes that agency goals are usually of a general nature, such as education of foster parents or support for one-parent families, while the worker's goals, as well as reflecting agency goals, will be more specific. She feels that the worker's goals will be related to the worker's assessment of members' capacities, needs and interests, and will be expressed through the worker's relationship with the members and participation in the group. The members' goals, however, are the expectations, hopes and objectives of each individual. These, Hartford (1972) suggests, may be overt and consistent with the agency's expressed goals or the members may not state their individual goals to the group. These unavowed needs may be unconscious. Hartford (1972) is also aware that some workers work to a 'hidden agenda', feeling that members will not participate if they are told that the worker's goal is to modify their attitudes or behaviour. She warns that for achievement of workers' and members' goals, members must be engaged in a process of formulation of goals and the development of the means to achieve them. For Garvin (1974), Hartford (1972) and Northern (1969) group goals seem to be initially established during the organizing period of the group through a process of interaction between agency, worker and members. As Northern (1969) notes: 'The purpose is a composite of the expressed purposes for the group held by the worker, and the expressed purposes of the members for the group' (p.105). The implication would seem to be that the workers and members are equally responsible for the establishment of overall group goals. In Northern's (1969) and Hartford's (1972) account of this process there seems to be little appreciation of the complexities and compromises which arriving at this composite might entail in some situations. Hartford (1972), however, does discuss the possibility of individuals leaving a group who were attracted to the initial agency goals but did not accept the composite goals which emerged as a result of group interaction processes.

Vinter (1967), however, sees the defining and harmonizing of goals, in ways that permit serving several clients through the same group's process, as a complex task. He suggests that either the worker can attempt to compose a group whose individual treatment goals are compatible, or define the purposes of the group in advance and select members with references to these so that adherence to these purposes becomes a condition of continued participation. Vinter (1967) suggests that groups vary in the amount of autonomy members have in determining their group goals. In contrast to the above example, Vinter states that in other situations broad purposes may be set for a group so that the members determine the specific ends within these limits.

Johnson and Johnson (1987), too, see the process as complex and ask whether group goals exist or are just a combination of individual goals. The literature probably needs to distinguish between general aims for the group which are provided by the group's initiator and in many instances agreed by the host agency, such as improve parenting skills, and more specific objectives such as responding appropriately to aggressive behaviour or understanding a child's developmental stages. The former are almost universally agreed before the group exists in any format, while the latter vary considerably in terms of workers' and members' input. This variation relates to the type of group under consideration. The process in a self-help group is likely to be very different from that of a treatment group. The style of the worker's role and agency policy will also effect the process. This is illustrated by the case study groups. In each case the general aims for the groups were either provided by the initiating worker or were part of a package used by this or another agency previously. There is more variation between the groups in terms of more specific objectives. The Girls' Group, the Men's Group for men who are the main carers of young children and the Positive Parenting Group all involved members in agreeing specific objectives, while the Anxiety Management had overt goals for individual members. In the Male Offenders' Group all objectives were predetermined.

Preston-Shoot (1987) and Benson (1987) clearly see the worker's role as defining the general purpose of the group as a starting-point. Preston-Shoot views subsequent discussions with members and information about resources available as the means of modifying the initial purpose and sharpening objectives. Whittaker (1985) sees the group leader having the responsibility for clarity on group aims. Benson's (1987) viewpoint is less clear. The importance of clarity of specific goals is stressed, both for the group as a whole and for individual members. This text implies that the worker's 'desired outcomes' may be broken down into specific objectives before the group begins and that the worker bases group goals on her or his assessment of the members. Other goals may be approved or negotiated with the members. It is not clear whether these member-agreed goals are group goals or individual goals. Both

Preston-Shoot (1987) and Benson (1987) emphasize the importance of clarity of aims among all group members and workers to aid group motivation towards objectives and to provide a yardstick by which to measure achievement.

The setting of overall group goals is perhaps more complex when the group is initiated as a community resource and members are not drawn from the worker's caseload or referred by other workers or agencies with the broad group aims in mind. In this situation members are often self-selecting, and the agency initiates the group having grounds for assuming some client need, the intention being that the worker and prospective members discuss whether the initial assumption of need was correct and, if so, translate this into an agreed group purpose or discuss alternative purposes if this is not acceptable to prospective members. This type of interaction to establish congruence of purposes can be extremely complex, since the agency goals may be fairly flexible but only within certain parameters, the prospective members have not yet committed themselves to the group and may decide not to join if the resulting goals are not acceptable, and members are likely to have different goals from each other. The resulting compromise may not fit agency policy or the leader's interests, and could take several weeks of discussion. This would seem to be a very different process to that described by Benson (1987) and Preston-Shoot (1987). To some extent the worker approaches of Mullender and Ward (1991) and Habermann (1990), described in Chapter 3, accord with this process. However, although the role of Mullender and Ward's worker is to enable members to articulate their own goals, the initial purpose of the group was already set. Brown (1994) echoes these processes in describing 'reciprocal approaches' in which the worker deliberately leaves the members to decide goals at the first meeting. Again, there is confusion about the purpose of the group and specific objectives for members.

A group set up by a Midlands voluntary agency began initially with the goal of setting up a group for isolated, depressed mothers in an inner-city tower block estate. The members were self-selecting, and after a few meetings the numbers dwindled into non-existence. The group was set up a second time and, after considerable discussion over a number of sessions, the purposes were revised to provide a supportive group for young mothers at home, mainly providing recreational activity with a focus on handicrafts. In this instance the agency regarded the redefined purposes as still within agency policy. Although there is a wide variety of opinion in the literature on how group goals are set, which is probably reflected in practice, there is considerable agreement that congruence between group members' aims and the group's overall goals is desirable, since it is closely related to member motivation and satisfaction, and group effectiveness.

Members' individual goals

Vernelle (1994) reminds us of the importance of each member to the group dynamics: '...there is no way for the individual to avoid influencing the group: even keeping silent can be a powerful contribution' (p.26). In the group planning stages, then, we need to attend to the objectives of individual members.

The literature discussed so far has not clearly specified the difference between individual goals and group goals. In much of the literature it is assumed that members and workers interact in the initial group stages to define overall group goals which are congruent with all the individual goals of the members. It is not always clear whether writers are assuming that, in addition to these agreed overall goals, individual goals are made explicit, either between member and worker or among the whole group. The differences between overall and individual goals are illustrated by the following example. A discussion on group purpose between a worker and potential members during the organizing period of the group might centre on whether a lunch club for ex-psychiatric patients should be a therapy group for the discussion of personal difficulties or a group offering support and companionship. Apart from these statements of possible overall group purposes, goals for individuals are often set and can be planned by the group as a whole or between member and worker. In the above example a member of the therapy group might have an individual goal of getting up by 9.00 a.m. every weekday, whereas the stated overall aim of the group might be to reintegrate the members back into the community by helping them to cope with day-to-day activities. Members may differ in the degree to which they feel they need specific goals and may bring up particular problems as they occur over time.

Levine (1967) stresses the importance of the pre-group interview between worker and prospective group member, in which the worker helps the client articulate individual goals, relates them to agency purpose and the goals of other group members as a preparation for the whole-group deliberation on purpose. In this situation, however, presumably the worker's goals are broadly defined before the interview and the prospective member has been selected from a caseload in relation to similarity of need to other members. Levine does mention a process of deliberation to establish a confluence of purposes, so it would seem that, although some deliberation is likely to take place on group purposes, considerable decisions on the worker's goals and individual goals, and the relationship between these, have been taken before the group members meet. In Boer and Lantz's (1974) adolescent therapy groups, individual therapeutic goals were specified during pre-group interviews between therapist, adolescent and parents, during which the broad group goals were also clarified. It would seem that in this group not only were group goals set by the therapists, but also individual goals were set in a private interview rather than as part of the group interaction. In common with Boer and Lantz (1974) and Levine (1967), Benson (1987) makes individual agreements with prospective members prior to the start of the group. These agreements seem to be aimed at ensuring that the member is clear about the purposes, processes and ground rules of the group, although mention is made of the members' individual needs and goals. Kamya (1997), in describing the preparation processes for groupwork with well children living with a family member who has AIDS, tells us that once it was established that the child itself did not have AIDS, an initial meeting was set up. This meeting was between the child, the family and the group workers. Its purpose was to provide more information about the group to the child and family, and to provide the workers with a better understanding of the child's background. This pre-group interview also began to address issues of confidentiality and the group contract. These pre-group interviews are clearly a prerequisite for two of the case study groups, the Positive Parenting Group and the Anxiety Management Group. Both group workers did home visits prior to the first meeting. The pre-meeting for the Anxiety Management Group was mainly to ascertain if the potential member's main concern was anxiety and whether they were motivated to work on it in a group. Individual goals were set, but this was in the final two weeks of the programme. In the Positive Parenting Group, individual goal setting was a two-part process which suggests the importance of this element to the workers. All potential members were invited to an introductory session at which they were asked to think about their personal goals. Subsequently home visits were made when individual goals were set between the worker and each member.

Motivation of members

Northern (1969) notes that 'both the effectiveness of the group and the satisfaction of its members are increased when the members perceive their personal aims as being advanced by the purpose of the group, when individual and group aims are perceived as being in harmony' (p.92). She also suggests that clarity of group purpose helps the member to perceive the advancement of personal aims, which therefore provides motivation towards the achievement of goals.

Vinter (1967) states that if there is discrepancy between members' and the worker's goals the worker may have to modify purposes for the group in order to achieve a higher degree of member involvement and motivation.

Hartford (1972) and Northern (1969) also stress that a worker's 'hidden agenda' or a member's unavowed aims can result in lack of congruence and therefore less member satisfaction and motivation. Vinter (1967) also relates readiness to change, motivation and the capacities of the member to the setting of individual goals. Douglas (1995), Vernelle (1994) and Johnson and Johnson (1987) are all concerned that members' hidden agendas can be very disruptive to the group. Johnson and Johnson (1987) describe them as 'personal goals that are unknown to all the other group members and are at cross-purposes with the dominant group goals' (p.139). For Douglas (1995), although he views the hidden agenda of members as possibly disruptive to effective group processes, he also views the unspoken aims of individuals as an inevitable part of group processes in that 'members, leaders and interested parties are all attempting to achieve outcomes for themselves and for the group and even for outsiders' (p.56). Vernelle (1994) feels that problems arise when important individual needs are not acknowledged by the other members. This, she suggests, leads to covert alliances and disguised items on the group agenda.

Workers, as well as members, have covert goals. While the Anxiety Management and the Positive Parenting Groups' workers and members have clearly agreed goals for individual group members, the Girls' Group and the Men's Group for men who are main carers of young children had no overt individual goals. However, in both instances the workers had covert goals for some members, using group processes to try to achieve these. In the former, the workers agreed goals for members which were not shared with the members. Chapter 2 details these goals, which mainly related to improving the social skills of some members and their social responses to others.

Contracting

The concepts of member identity and involvement with group goal setting, and its relationship with group members' motivation, is closely related to the concept of contract negotiation. The concept of contract assumes that the member and worker are responsible to each other to fulfil agreements on tasks and goals so that the member is an active self-determining individual who consciously and deliberately co-operates in the intervention process. The implication is that if the member takes responsibility for choosing goals, this will enhance motivation and investment in the intervention process, and the member may experience a sense of identity with effective outcomes.

Brown (1994), Benson (1987), Houston (1990) and Rutan and Stone (1984) discuss agreeing contracts between all group members and workers. Benson (1987) thinks workers should make many contracts with individual members as well as with the group as a whole. This is central to Benson's group planning processes: '...the group contract is vital to ensure that members understand what is being asked of them and can agree to pursue particular objectives. Articulation of goals at the individual and collective level develops consensus' (p.100). Kamya's (1997) group for well children living with a family member with AIDS begins to discuss the group contract before members join the group. The contract is then stated explicitly at the first group meeting for each member. This, it is felt, enables existing members to revisit the contract, illustrating the parameters of the group and stressing the necessity of confidentiality. It is felt to be particularly important here because of effects on the wider community.

Most of these principles of user responsibility and identity are discussed in the literature on goal setting in groupwork, but the 'contract' approach, particularly, highlights some of the possible effects of increased member clarity and involvement in goal setting.

Garvin (1974) has applied Reid and Epstein's (1972) 'task-centred' casework model to work with groups. In this analysis group goal setting is achieved by a number of processes: an array of problems the member would like to work on in the group is elicited; these problems are defined behaviourally, and here members help each other to make the information more explicit; members rank their own problems in order of priority; and the target problem is then determined by the collaborative effort of the member, the worker and the other members. As in Reid and Epstein's (1972) model, the problem the member is most interested in resolving is normally the one selected. The complexities which could arise are foreseen by Garvin (1974), since he suggests that members may decide to work on particular problems because of their similarity or dissimilarity to those of other group members, or the worker may suggest an order of preference if this will facilitate the identification of tasks together. In this way goal setting via explicit member–worker–co-member contracts is related to member motivation and group effectiveness. This has similarities, but is in fact a rather different approach, to the behaviourally defined user issues in the Anxiety Management Group. Here, the worker's initial assessment and the subsequent setting of individual goals are not seen as part of the group processes for other members. Rather, this is a set of interactions between the worker and member alone.

Reassessment and Evaluation

Although most of the discussion in the literature is concerned with initial goal setting, there is widespread acknowledgement (for example, Hartford 1972) that group goals may later be re-examined or assessed. Hartford states that goals may be modified as the group changes focus or as the group changes composition, particularly if it is an open-ended group. This is more likely if the group is long term. A change of worker in the Girls' Group provided an opportunity for the group as a whole to redefine the group purposes in more user-friendly language.

The relationship between clarity of group goals and evaluation of group effectiveness is discussed by Benson (1987), Hartford (1972) and Vinter (1967). Hartford (1972) suggests that the establishment of clear goals provides the framework for the assessment of group activities as a means towards these clarified goals. Benson (1987) suggests that goals are a way of evaluating the effectiveness of group procedures. Vinter (1967) suggests that specific individual goals within the agreed group goals should be defined in concrete and behaviourally specific terms, so that movement towards these goals can be more definitely assessed.

Summary

It would seem that there are a wide variety of ways in which group goals are established in relation to the levels of participation in goal setting for the agency, the worker and the group members. These levels range along a continuum of practice, from the Male Offenders' Group, in which the worker defined the group goals in advance and selected members with reference to these, to the Positive Parenting Group, where members set individual goals which then became part of the group agenda within the agreed group purpose.

Not only are there wide variations in the levels of responsibility for setting goals among the participants, there are also differences in the degree to which specific individual goals are set in addition to overall group goals. These differences would seem to be due to differing policies of agencies and attitudes of both workers and members, which in turn may be related to such factors as the type of group set-up, the type of agency, and the age of the members. It would seem more likely that groups set up by medical agencies would be viewed as treatment groups by the worker and members, having fairly specific aims and selection criteria and probably little member participation in the setting of group or individual goals. It could be that there is a similar tendency for groups set up for children or adolescents, in that they are seen as recipients rather than participants and therefore not capable of participating in goal setting. The length of time the group runs is possibly also an important factor since members who have developed considerable cohesion and patterns of leadership may feel able to reassess group goals in ways which they feel to be appropriate. There appears at present to be no research into the varieties of practice of group goal setting or the possible causal factors involved. There is, however, considerable agreement in the literature on the importance of clarity of goals due to its relationship to a variety of preparation processes. This includes assessment and evaluation of ongoing group processes, and effective outcome. The value of congruence between workers' and members' goals is also widely acknowledged, since there is often a close association between congruence and members' motivation towards, and identification with, group goals, which may result in greater member satisfaction and more effective outcomes.

Chapter 5

Physical Environments

The importance of the environment in which groups are held has perhaps received less attention than any other area of preparation for groupwork. The factors relating to the physical environment in which groups are held, with which practitioners may be concerned, would seem to be threefold:

1. the degree to which group members identify the environment with a particular agency or institution, and the possible effects of this identification on member commitment and motivation

2. the suitability of the environment for the planned activities of a group

3. the possible effects of the physical provision on group tasks, members' attitudes and behaviour.

Of these three 1 and 2 are the environmental factors to which most practitioners give attention. There is an obvious overlap between all three areas and in the following discussion they will be treated together. Literature related to the third factor is mainly taken from the field of environmental psychology.

Identity and suitability

The organizers of the practice groups had clearly considered some of these three elements in their planning stages.

The youth service's Girls' Group was deliberately held in the community centre because it was important that the girls identify their use of the centre with the group's positive activities and use of the male-dominated equipment, so that they would continue to use these in a mixed-group situation.

The occupational therapist organizing the Anxiety Management Group held it in the community mental health teamroom. She thought this was not entirely suitable for the group's purpose since the room was too small for the relaxation exercises, although good for the group teaching element. In terms of members' identity, the room was felt to be less stigmatized than a hospital setting, but the presence of a residential mental health unit next door was felt possibly to stigmatize the venue.

The social services' Men's Group for men who are main carers of young children's venue was chosen with care. The workers decided not to hold the group in social services premises in case this had any negative identities for members. Instead the group was held in a family centre, known to two of the members. The room was comfortable, furnished for adults and was felt to have a relaxing ethos. The workers thought it to be very suitable for the purpose.

The probation service Male Offenders' Group was deliberately held on probation service premises since it was intended to foster a positive image of the service. The room was large and comfortable with a pool table, and tea and coffee making facilities. It was felt to be a relaxed environment and very appropriate for the purpose.

The Positive Parenting Group used the family centre dining-room. This was usually used as a coffee and social room by centre users and so was seen as a relaxing environment. It was also large enough for people to sit out of the group to have private conversations, thus providing some user choice. It was felt to be very suitable for this group.

The Women's Group and the Anger Management Group were both held in the same agency group room. Both workers saw this as a large, comfortable room with sufficient space for members to move around during the group. Its separation from the rest of the building was also seen to be important in terms of implying a separation of function from the centre's other activities.

The Women's Mental Health Group meetings are held in the clients' lounge. The size of the room and its level of comfort were seen to be important variables here.

All the practice groups, to varying degrees, considered all three elements of the physical context of their group and the effects of these on group outcomes. Clearly, the range of choice of environment was not very great for organizers but, since they were aware of the issues, the best use could be made of what was available.

Fatout and Rose (1995), in planning task groups, view place and physical environment as exceedingly important and requiring careful planning. Environments are seen as affecting members' interactions. They stress the importance of structural features, such as position of stairs and lifts, and walking distance.

Konopka (1963) states that 'physical surroundings are consciously planned' and that 'the conscious use or creation of environment...[is a] part of the group work process' (p.75). Konopka gives three examples of ways in which particular environments are symbolic or may be identified by members as an agency or type of intervention. An outpatient group for adult epileptics, who needed help with social relations since many of them had spent most of their lives isolated at home, was held in the hospital. This was planned deliberately in order to symbolize that the group was part of the treatment plan. Konopka (1963) warns that, although school buildings are often offered to groups as premises after school hours, they are inappropriate for groups of children with school problems since, however unlike school the group is, the children are likely to identify it with school, and group purposes are unlikely to be achieved. Konopka's (1963) third example describes an experiment with some 'unclubbable' boys in London. The boys met with their club leader on a moving river barge. The barge was like a home in that they 'looked after' it, and it provided them with a vehicle for adventurous exploits. The fact that these 'unclubbable' boys enjoyed, and stayed with, the club was probably partly due to the added excitement of being on a barge. It may also be that the boys did not identify the barge as an official 'youth club' provided by authority figures for their improvement.

In some situations it may be, as in Konopka's (1963) first example, that identification of various kinds can be used in positive ways. This is certainly the intention of the probation service in our Male Offenders' Group. However, it may be an area to which little thought is given and premises for groups may be chosen because they are convenient and available. It may not always be an issue of any consequence but, in situations where members are likely to make identifications, practitioners may find it useful to assess whether these identifications are congruent with group goals. For example, groups which are encouraging the rehabilitation into the community of long-term psychiatric patients may feel the goals are best served by meeting in premises less identifiable as 'hospital', such as the student nurses' TV room or a staff house on the edge of the hospital grounds. A group whose main aim is to remove the stigma from parents of 'looked-after' children may consider very carefully whether meetings should be held in social services offices. It may be that the practitioner in the above group would decide that given the identification, gains are to be made by using social services premises, but the important factor in all these cases is that possible identification should be seen as a factor in decision making about environments for groups.

Brown (1994) and Douglas (1995) discuss environment in relation to the ethos of particular agencies and agency premises, and their possible identities for individual users. They acknowledge that such identities need not be negative but that the use of neutral territory should be a consideration.

Konopka (1963) considers that key elements which need to be conveyed to group members by the provision of physical environments are related to privacy for the group. This provides a sense of intimacy, and the acceptance of members as individuals with worth, whose needs are considered with care. An example of how these elements could be conveyed to members, partly through physical provision, is given in the description of the group for epileptics mentioned above. The group met in a comfortable living-room so that patients could get used to a social, informal situation. The chairs were arranged so that members could see each other, but not in a rigid circle, and some chairs were placed at the side with small tables containing magazines. These outer chairs were to enable shyer members to withdraw when they needed to, without being too obvious. Food and coffee was also arranged, to have something for their hands to do. The relationship between physical provision and the group aims can also be clearly seen here. This need to provide some space for members to sit apart at times, or to move around the room, is also illustrated by the Anger Management and Positive Parenting Groups.

Parsloe (1971) and Hartford (1972), in common with Fatout and Rose (1995), stress the importance of always holding a group meeting in the same room, since the room comes to have certain meanings for the members. Hartford (1972) notes that the group's location reinforces group consciousness and its familiarity provides continuity and orientation. Parsloe (1971) reports that a group which changed rooms after meeting for a year 'seemed to go back to the fragmented kind of talk which had characterised our first few meetings' (p.55). Fatout and Rose (1995) see members building a sense of identity with the meeting-room, which contributes to group cohesion and becomes related to the achievement of group activities. Brown (1994) sees familiar territory as having a reassuring function.

Davies (1975, p.93), contrasting a formal discussion group with an informal mothers' group, suggests that the physical environment, together with the prescription relating to the use of that environment, effected the nature of the meeting and relationships within the group. The rigid circle of chairs in the Girls' Group would not seem to encourage informal relationships in the group or spontaneous, relaxed contributions. The informal seating arrangements with the freedom to sit, stand or move about the room in the mothers' group would seem more conducive to informal friendly conversation and informal friendly relationships between members and between workers and members. Hunter, Bailey and Taylor (1996) comment on the effects of the layout of chairs for a co-operative group meeting. Brown and Clough (1989), in analysing groups in residential child-care settings, acknowledge the importance of the room layout, and position of chairs and other furniture, in effecting the level and type of interactions between children, and children and staff. Brown (1994) is very aware of physical layouts and their suitability for the tasks required.

It is difficult, however, to look at the effect of physical environments in isolation, since group outcomes are the results of many interacting factors, including the physical provision. The type of environment provided often reflects the style of leadership and the type of group the worker wishes to initiate, whether or not the worker is conscious of pursuing a particular group ethos.

Churchill (1959) is also aware that group environments can be planned in order to encourage particular group activity. In describing a therapy group for boys, she states that 'total room arrangement can also be used to control the amount of gross physical activity desired' (p.56). In one session a mat was placed on the floor. The children had accepted the rule that they could never play on the mat with shoes on. By placing the mat on the floor, the worker intended to limit hyperactive running and encourage the group to exert self-control. A hanging rope was used to encourage interaction between the boys. Boys found it difficult to climb or swing on the rope alone. They were therefore obliged to work in pairs, taking turns pushing and swinging. A barrel was similarly used to encourage interaction. Over time, the barrel on its side had come to be used for two boys to play in. Its introduction to any session formed part of the worker's planned activities. The relationship between the arrangement of the room and the type of activity which might be encouraged is clearly shown by Churchill's (1959) examples. Hall's (1974, p.51) description of the reception area of a children's department takes up Konopka's (1963) point that the type of environment provided for the client will be perceived as indicative of the agency's attitude to users. In this example the agency did not seem to hold the consumers in high esteem.

Beyond groupwork literature itself, there has been some discussion in related social care texts of the effects of physical environment on outcome, the closest context being residential care. Ainsworth and Fulcher (1981) state: 'The siting and physical design of a centre plus the spatial arrangements of rooms and furnishings all play a fundamental part in determining how a group care environment is enacted' (p.183). This theme is further expanded in Fulcher and Ainsworth (1985). Slater and Lipman (1980, p.220), in analysing the design and internal layout of a number of residential homes for older people, have provided a checklist of questions by which we can focus on the desired outcomes of particular design elements.

Design element   **Desired outcome**

Does the design of this:

Neighbourhood
Building   Activity, Mobility, Self-care,
Room   Independence, Social participation,
Wall   **facilitate**   Privacy, Personalization, Dignity,
Floor   Security, Stimulation, Choice,
Furniture   Familiarity, Self-determination?
Fitment

Group tasks, members' attitudes and behaviours

Some useful contributions to this literature can be drawn from the field of environmental psychology. Theoretical and empirical perspectives on the relationship between physical environment and behaviour began to appear in various forms from the early 1970s. Sociologists, however, had begun to study the relationship between behaviour and environment in the late 1950s and 1960s in the form of socio-technical systems; that is, the patterns of interaction between men and production technology (see, for example, Blauner 1963).

Perhaps the most significant development in this area has been the evolution of environmental psychology as a field of study. An edited volume of readings published (Proshansky, Ittelson and Rivlin 1976) defined its main role as the definition of the substantive and conceptual boundaries of the field of environmental psychology. This is now a well-established international field of study. Cantor's (1991) contribution to the 22nd Annual Conference of the Environmental Design Research Association, held in Mexico, draws up a model that considers the human use of space and human responses to place experience. Veitch and Arkkelin (1995) acknowledge the contributions to this field from a range of disciplines: 'Environmental Psychology constitutes an area of enquiry that is rooted in numerous disciplines...[that] share an interest in understanding the...set of relationships between humans and their environment' (p.4).

The theoretical frameworks and research findings taken from environmental psychology on the whole have not been generally related to groupwork; however, their importance to groupwork planners lies in the fact that they are attempting to establish a relationship between physical environment and behaviour. The most relevant areas of this field are:

- concepts of personal space – this includes privacy and territoriality
- room design
- design of public-use buildings and their environs.

Personal space

Gifford (1987) explores the concept of personal space in terms of appropriate distance and crowding. He states that the concept is common to all human beings and that differences are personal, situational and cultural. Inappropriate spacing, he states, leads to discomfort, lack of protection, stress, anxiety and poor communication, while appropriate spacing usually has positive outcomes.

Cave (1998), in common with Veitch and Arkkelin (1995), also explores the concept of what is a comfortable distance from others, as well as what and how people perceive private territory such as their own homes (primary territory). Fuhrer, Kaiser and Hartig (1993) researched the relationship between attachment to home and nearby home territories, and mobility to leisure activities. They found that the higher the attachment to home territory, the lower the mobility rates to leisure activities. Of interest to us is that they found that place attachment was based on affective meanings inhabitants attached to physical aspects of home and near-home territories, rather than the purely physical qualities of these territories. Oseland and Donald's (1993) research showed that a person's evaluation of space in their home is, among other variables, related to satisfaction with the level of privacy available. This satisfaction was distinguished from the amount of space provided. Gutheil (1992) discusses the influence of physical space on behaviour and how an understanding of this can aid social work practice. The importance of territory, personal space, crowding and privacy are emphasized.

Newman (1972), in his concept of 'defensible space', claimed that it is possible to create a physical living environment that both inhabitant and stranger will perceive to be an area under the undisputed influence of the inhabitants, and that the inhabitants dictate who uses it and for what purposes. The main factor here is that such territory should afford good visual surveillance to the inhabitants. This 'living environment' refers not only to houses or flats, but to areas around the property such as paths, yards and communal staircases which are often treated as no one's particular responsibility. He suggested that physical design can change this attitude. Ham-Rawbottom, Gifford and Kelly (1999), in reviewing defensible space theories, applied these concepts to the vulnerability of houses to burglary. Although elements other than those included in defensible space schema were also identified as aspects of vulnerability, the former were seen to be likely predictors of house vulnerability to burglars. Abu-Ghazzeh (1999), in his study of site design around multiple-family housing units and social interaction, found that the level of social interaction and friendship formation related to the design of the environment around the housing units. This needed to provide opportunities for residents to walk around a small group of houses and to sit in small, confined spaces which became small semi-private courtyards.

Veitch and Arkkelin (1995) discuss the concept of secondary territory. These are territories over which people feel they have some degree of perceived ownership. This may be temporary, in that they don't have total control of the territory, or they may be in control for only short periods of time. This is a useful concept for group workers since groups which meet in the same room each week are likely to acquire just this sort of secondary ownership of this territory. Fatout and Rose (1995), in their discussion of task groups, emphasize the importance of recognizing this.

The concepts of crowding, privacy and territory are essential elements for group planners to consider when planning the context in which the group will take place. The Positive Parenting Group and the Women's Group both illustrate that these elements were part of their planning processes. The Women's Group were concerned that the room have sufficient space for the participants to be able to move around the room during the group meeting. The Positive Parenting Group wanted a room large enough for people to sit out of the group to have private conversations.

Room design

Cave (1998) and Gifford (1987), in reviewing the literature on room design, examine Osmond's (1959) concepts of sociopetal and sociofugal seating arrangements. Sociopetal settings facilitate social interaction, while sociofugal settings discourage social interaction. A sociopetal seating arrangement would be illustrated by members of a meeting sitting around an oval table, so that all members could communicate with each other. An example of a sociofugal seating arrangement would be rows of fixed seating in an airport lounge, arranged so that occupants face away from each other. Cave (1998) gives as further examples of sociofugal seating church pews and shopping centre seats with their backs to one another. Osmond (1959) notes from his work in a psychiatric hospital that chairs in rows or along walls seemed to prevent conversation, whereas chairs arranged around small tables or facing each other in small groups seemed to increase the number of conversations. These arrangements, however, need to fit the purpose of the seating. If seating needs to provide privacy, as in a library, or anonymity, as in a public waiting room, then a sociofugal design may well be the most appropriate.

A major contribution to our understanding of the various effects of seating arrangements on the participants has been made by Sommer (1969). In an early experiment in which people were given a choice of seats in a cafeteria, he found that people who were working on a co-operative venture chose seats side by side. Competitive people chose opposite seating, while corner positions which provided physical proximity and visual contact were most popular with those who wanted to talk. Sommer's suggestion that 'opposite' seating is related to competitive activity may mean that circular seating arrangements so often used by discussion and psychotherapy groups may not be the most advantageous. Sommer, Wong and Cook (1992) returned to reassess an experiment begun in 1972. Here a university classroom had been designed with carpeted floor, fabric wall coverings and soft-covered seats, to make the room more aesthetically pleasing and therefore more encouraging of student interaction. It became known as the soft classroom and the earlier experiment had shown its design to be more conducive to interaction than traditional classrooms. A survey completed in 1991 showed that the room continued to enhance student participation relative to straight-row classrooms.

Wools and Canter (1970) conducted a systematic series of experiments to determine some of the variables involved in judgements concerned with the 'friendliness' of rooms. The variables concerned were seating arrangements, ceiling angle (sloping or horizontal) and window shape. The findings demonstrated that the room with a sloping ceiling was perceived as more 'friendly' than the horizontal one, and that certain seating arrangements could endow a room with 'friendliness'.

Group workers are often unable to affect the choice of group room, but research into the possible effects on behaviour of the internal design elements, such as chair layouts, space to move around or designs which encourage greater direct interaction, can be planned in relation to a particular group's goals.

Experiments which monitor the effect of the design of play equipment on the interaction levels of young children offer us additional insights. An experiment by Smith (1974) would seem to provide evidence to support Churchill's (1959) work. The experiment in a playgroup compared play sessions with large objects, such as a Wendy House or toy box, with similar sessions where jigsaws, tea-sets and toy telephones were available. The former produced more talking, more physical contact, more gross motor activity and more co-operation. The study therefore suggests that co-operative behaviour might be induced by changing the type of physical play equipment. Hayward *et al.* (1974) conducted a study in New York to compare children's activities in three types of playground: a traditional playground with fixed steel apparatus; an 'adventure' playground; and a 'contemporary' playground with some aspects of the other two types of playground. The results suggested that 'loose' materials – that is, those that could be changed and combined – produced more peer interaction and verbal communication than other play activities.

The type of equipment provided and its likely effect on the kinds of interactions between participants links to Chapter 6. This is particularly well illustrated by the Girls' Group's choice of equipment. Here equipment is selected not only to encourage interaction but also to illustrate that girls can enjoy and succeed with activities seen as the main province of the boy users.

Public-use buildings and environs

The design of public buildings and their environs was of particular interest to early writers on environmental psychology (for example, Canter 1974; Proshansky *et al.* 1976). In this sector the design of hospitals, schools, prisons, libraries, museums and residential homes were analysed in terms of how the design features affected the users, and suggestions were made to improve the buildings' functioning for both user and staff. Slater and Lipman (1980), for example, in their research on 12 residential units for older people, found that: the circular design of corridors added to the confusion of some residents; the smallness of rooms meant that residents could not invite friends into their rooms so that all social interaction was in public spaces; and the provision of toilets in central blocks meant residents had usually to be taken there by a member of staff. Cave (1998) and Gifford (1987) provide good summaries of these research findings. Veitch and Arkkelin (1995) provide a similar diagram to Slater and Lipman's (p.317):

Important concepts:

Hospital Design	patient vs staff needs
	individual differences
	efficiency and radial designs
	privacy and control
Residential Care Facilities	single vs multiple stories
	passive outdoor recreation
	landscape considerations
	table and fountain height
	dining area considerations
	multipurpose auditoriums
	colour coding
	stairway risers/handrails
	living quarters issues
Philosophies of Prison Design	classroom position and participation
	position and seminar participation
	illumination
	room colour and emotion
	open-space classrooms: noise, distraction, privacy
	user-environment congruence
	design criteria: profit, quality, performance, competition, flexibility, elegance, safety, time.

Kerr and Tacon's (1999) research suggests that entering buildings induces particular psychological states. The findings suggest that individuals are sensitive to the psychological states required in particular settings.

Although the design of the building is unlikely to be within the control of the group worker, consideration needs to be given to the effect of the design of the building and its environs, since these need to be regarded as some of the interactive elements which may have consequences for group outcomes.

Chapter 6

Activities and Group Programmes

Introduction

The purpose of social groupwork is to bring about some kind of change in its group members through the medium of group interaction. Those who select group activities are concerned with selecting experiences or ways of interacting most likely to bring about the type of change needed by the individual members and which meet overall group goals. As Phyllida Parsloe (1971) notes: 'Activity is a means to helping members relate to each other' (p.45). All activity in a group can be viewed as member interaction and therefore as a means of attaining goals. This could include informal chats before the group begins, serving the coffee, getting out equipment or discussing travel arrangements for the following session.

These groups, unlike leisure- or task-centred groups such as tenants' associations, are not set up with the activity as their prime objective, but activities are used as a means of achieving the group's objectives. A group for people with mental health problems may select activities which particularly encourage members to relate to each other and to the group workers where poor social interaction is seen to be a difficulty. All such groups engage in some type of activity which could focus mainly on discussion, handicrafts, users' contributions or a pre-set order of exercises. Group organizers have to make judgements about what activities a particular group will engage in which will be most likely to achieve the goals for the group.

The relationship between agreed group goals and a group's activities is not always very apparent. Activities often seem to be selected because the available meeting space will only accommodate particular activities or because a particular focus is traditional for the agency or the professions of the group workers.

Davies (1975), in his discussion of how leaders choose a group's activities, says 'decisions about what a group should do and evaluations of what it has done seem repeatedly to rely on untested and often highly subjective assumptions' (p.65). He suggests that, rather than carefully matching the needs of the individual with the specific activity, workers are more likely to select some form of discussion, outdoor pursuits or community service, all three of which, he states, have been largely uncritically accepted for use in group situations. Davies is particularly critically of the widespread use of discussion as a central focus for many groups: 'Verbal exchanges with clients conducted one at a time are thereby replaced by verbal exchanges carried on with a number of clients simultaneously.' (p.65) He suggests that verbal exchange is a method with which the worker feels comfortable and its use as the focus for groupwork is an extension of individual work rather than a focus chosen for the greatest effect. Davies admits that groups engage in activities other than these three, but he suggests that the basis for choice bears no relation to the group's aims or the needs of the individual group members.

Davies's (1975) criticism of practitioners may be too harsh, but problems do arise for practitioners in selecting specific activities to achieve particular objectives. This has been hampered by the lack of analytical frameworks.

Frameworks for practitioners

A number of writers provide a comprehensive range of games and exercises for practitioners to use. Some of the most well known of these are Priestley and Maguire (1984) and Brandes and Phillips (1977). Butler and Wintram (1991) and Houston (1990) provide details of exercises within the text, while Hunter (1992) and Hickson (1995) provide lists of games and exercises. Hickson (1995) divides the exercises into four sections: drama games, psychodrama, dramatherapy, theatre of the oppressed and ritual. Each of these games has aims, timings, preparation, action, procedure and closure approaches. Similarly, Hunter provides 95 exercises, each with similar directions. An extremely comprehensive chapter in Dwivedi (1993) provides a summary of different approaches to group activities. This does include the use of games but also provides some theoretical approaches that underlie some examples of social groupwork.

These include: cognitive behavioural therapy approaches, transactional analysis approaches and humanistic approaches.

Analytical approaches

While the provision of games and exercises often includes a general objective for each game, it does not provide an analytical framework which can analyse all aspects of group processes.

In the 1950s, Gump and Sutton-Smith (1955) began to examine the relationship between particular types of behaviour and particular activities in children. Their observations and research suggested that the precise impact of an activity on the participants is partly determined by who takes part but also by the demands and limitations which the essential structure of that activity imposes on them.

These authors hypothesize that

> activities have a reality and a behaviour influencing power in their own right. An activity area entered will exclude some potential behaviours, necessitate other behaviours and finally encourage or discourage still other behaviours.

The essential structure of the activity will elicit particular 'respondent behaviours'.

This can be illustrated by describing the effects of two different but similar games on 'Freddy':

> At first Freddy refused to play the game; later he was persuaded to play. In the 'it' role he was at first reluctant and uncertain: then he experienced moderate success. With each capture of a tail his stance was more confident, his chasing more vigorous; finally as his tension melted away he began to laugh... The game ingredient which contributed to Freddy's pleasurable experience was that of a Central Person role which had considerable game-giver power, 'it' was free of game retaliation. This 'it' role required only a moderate amount of physical competence, an amount which Freddy possessed.

> In the second game, a cat attempts to catch a mouse. A circled group joins hands and attempts to block the cat and protect the mouse. Freddy becomes the cat and is initially excited and assertive. But he has no success... Freddy blusters that he will use a 'special trick' but the trick doesn't work. Freddy scowls...after several more hopeless attempts,

Freddy, in a sullen temper, quits the game. (Gump and Sutton-Smith 1955, p.263)

A research study by Gump and Sutton-Smith (1955) tested the hypothesis that *'the amount and kind of social interaction is significantly affected by the variation of activity-settings'* (p.756). The subjects were 23 boys aged nine-and- a-half to eleven-and-a-half years, at a summer camp, referred there because of some adjustment difficulties. The report findings concern swimming and craft activities. Types of social interaction were divided into six categories: sharing, helping, asserting, blocking, demanding and attacking. The amount of overall interaction was noted as well as the persons involved in types of interaction. The results are shown in Table 6.1.

Table 6.1 A summary of interactions		
	Swim	**Craft**
Average number of overall interactions	38.8	26.4
% interaction between boys and staff	26	46

The predominant staff/boy interactions in swim were 'sharing' followed by 'conflict' (34 per cent, made up of a combination of 'demand', 'block' and 'attack'). 'Conflict' was 17 per cent in craft staff/boy interactions. These results indicate that in swim the staff members were involved in few helping interactions but were called on to settle conflicts. In craft, the staff role was mainly helping. Peer interactions also differed between activities. Swim seems to encourage high peer interaction, high assertion and attack. Craft seems to encourage low peer interaction with minimal peer conflict interaction. This research investigates the characteristics of these two activities in terms of likely respondent behaviours. It does not attempt to investigate particular effects on participants with known individual needs.

Vinter (1974) revised and extended Gump and Sutton-Smith's (1955) conception in his attempt to formulate a framework for the analysis of all activities used in social groupwork. Like them, he states that all activities comprise an 'activity setting' which is likely to evoke certain 'respondent behaviours' in the participants. Vinter's main contribution to activity analysis is his six dimensions of activity-setting framework, which is a schema for analysing the 'activity setting' of all activities in order to predict the likely 'respondent behaviour' of participants. Vinter (1974) claims that all group activity can be analysed using this framework. He suggests each dimension can be graded high, medium or low for each activity. Vinter's six dimensions are given below, with illustrations from our case studies.

PRESCRIPTIVENESS *The degree of prescribed structure for an activity, e.g. a game of snooker would have high prescriptiveness*

Activities in the Women's Mental Health Group are a repeat of a well-tested model and would score high for prescriptiveness since each activity is set and timed for a particular session.

The Positive Parenting Group's activities would score medium for prescriptiveness since the leader has set a general framework for each session but participants can change the content to meet their own needs or approach the same content by user-agreed means.

CONTROLS *Level of staff control in the activity, e.g. technique instruction, provision of tools, materials*

The Men's Group for men who are main carers of young children would score low for controls, since the users agree, manage and change the activities themselves.

Controls would seem high for the Male Offenders' Group since staff retain and manage control of the exercises and materials needed for each exercise.

COMPETENCE *Level needed to take part, e.g. a low level for free play, a high level for portrait painting*

The adult survivors of the Anger Management Group can be scored as medium for competence, since participants need to be able to communicate effectively with the group as a whole, and feel able to share their personal feelings and experiences, within a group.

It seems likely that motivation will also relate to competence to take part, in the Men's Group for men who are main carers of young children. Given a reasonable level of motivation, competence here scores as medium since the activities are clearly user devised.

INTERACTION *Verbal or non-verbal, ranging from high level, e.g. a football game, a shared group task, to low level, e.g. a lone activity with little need of staff response*

Interaction would score high for the Positive Parenting Group where the verbal interactions are constant and parents are keen to make and listen to other contributions.

The Male Offenders' Group is less interactive, since verbal contributions are more spasmodic and reflective; however, non-verbal interaction is sometimes high. A medium score.

REWARDS *Both to members and how widely they are distributed in the group, e.g. personal achievement, group identity, public achievement*

Rewards are complex and at a number of levels and are therefore quite difficult to score for the case study groups. Some of these groups have member self-evaluation pro formas or verbal feedback. The former tend to score high on rewards although this formal process is unlikely to cover the spectrum of personal rewards. The latter tends to produce a more varied, critical response.

MOVEMENT *The amount of physical movement required*

This dimension scores low for all our case studies except the Girls' Group, which scores high. However, it is an important dimension for members with disabilities or participants who need to be physically active.

The schema does not in general attempt to analyse respondent behaviour, although Vinter (1974) does predict likely behaviours under each dimension for craft and swim activities. The framework does not relate respondent behaviour to individual needs, or to group or individual goals. It is the practitioner who must use Vinter's framework to analyse the likely reward for participants and to relate this to individual group goals.

Whittaker (1974) has attempted to extend Vinter's (1974) framework by relating the six dimensions to eight types of children. It was initiated for use in a residential children's setting so that the activity examples are mainly of the 'games' variety. Davies (1975) used Vinter's six dimensions to analyse likely 'respondent behaviours in a social group work setting'. Davies contrasts the two types of discussion group for women, one formal and the other informal. He applies Vinter's (1974) framework to all activities which occur in the meetings, including arriving and departing, provision of refreshments and the amount of physical contact permitted.

Davies's (1975) interpretation of Vinter's (1974) framework highlights the importance of analysing all aspects of group interaction, since all elements affect participant perception and therefore the group's effectiveness.

Gump and Sutton-Smith (1955), Vinter (1974) and Whittaker (1974) all use activities with children as examples, swim and craft being predominant. Vinter claims that all activities can be analysed using his framework to predict likely respondent behaviour.

A wider application of the framework

In order to test the above claim, Phillips (1989) used Vinter's (1974) framework to analyse a wider range of activities in a day centre for adults recovering from mental illness. In this centre new members meet with staff to discuss their goals and to choose activities which meet these needs. This discussion forms an initial contract which is reviewed in four weeks.

The activities selected were badminton, arts and crafts, the Tuesday Group, a repairs workshop, washing up and clearing away.

Each activity was observed on four separate occasions by the author and the manager, each making separate readings. Vinter's (1974) framework was used and a high, medium or low measure for each dimension was recorded. Judgement decisions between the author and the manager on the measures were in agreement.

The Tuesday Group is a weekly discussion group in which members' personal problems and coping strategies are discussed as well as aspects of running the day centre. In the first half of the session, the whole group meets. In the second half, members are in small groups with a staff member to each group. This type of discussion structure provides controlled, highly prescriptive activity which encourages high interaction between all participants in the second half, with low interaction in the first half, and that being mainly staff/member.

Badminton seems also to be a controlled, prescriptive activity, but medium competence levels were well tolerated in this setting and interaction (verbal and non-verbal) for all participants was medium to high.

Arts and crafts was more complex to analyse than the other activities, since high, medium or low scores for interaction for staff/participant and participant/participant varied according to the tasks in this mixed task group.

Washing up and clearing away was a prescriptive and controlled activity which seemed to require medium competence and to encourage interaction as long as the tasks within the activity were shared. The latter was also partly dependent on the physical design of the kitchen. Socially valued in the day centre, it provides rewards for all participants.

The repairs workshop mends an item each week. Usually the member of staff and one to three members are involved in the repair, the rest of the group congregate around this activity and discuss the repair and/or general topics. Scores on the dimensions therefore vary. 'Whole group' describes those not actually involved in the repair. The activity seems to be rewarding for all in the group. It is less controlled and prescriptive for the non-repairers and therefore may well be attractive to members who find it difficult to join in more formal sessions.

This application of Vinter's framework highlights its usefulness in differentiating between respondents' behaviours where participants are engaged on different tasks within an apparently similar activity; for example, arts and crafts, oil painting and puppet making. It highlights differences in working in pairs/small groups on a shared activity, working in pairs on the same activity, and working in a group on one's own activity.

There is a tendency for dimensions to be blanket descriptions. They may need more behavioural-specific definitions. It seems likely that particular settings will need to be more specific for some dimensions than others in relation to unit objectives and individual and small-group goals. In the day centre for the recovering mentally ill, interaction was the most useful dimension. However, when applied as a differentiator between activities and elements of activities it was found not to distinguish between negative and positive interactions. Gump and Sutton-Smith (1955) define six types of social interaction which Vinter (1974) has not incorporated into his framework.

Van der Ven's (1985) concept of appropriate time dimension in activity programmes focuses on the importance of giving participants sufficient time to complete a task satisfactorily to ensure participant reward. Van der Ven also focuses on understimulation and overstimulation, or setting the activity at an appropriate participant level. Each of these elements could be incorporated into Vinter's competence and reward dimension to provide further classification and refinement.

The application of Vinter's (1974) framework to participants in a day centre for adults recovering from mental illness suggests it may well have wide-ranging applicability in residential, day care and other social groupwork contexts. It would seem, however, that the framework needs refining to differentiate a wider range of respondent behaviour. It may well also need the adoption of some specific dimensions to provide analysis in some settings. In its present form, however, it provides a framework which can be applied to give overall guidelines in the choice of activities and their likely indicators of participant response, in order to achieve users' goals more reliably.

The flexibility of group activities

The degree to which a group's activities are flexible or pre-set varies considerably. Some agencies run a particular group over a long period of time. This may be a specific model which another agency has piloted or it may be a model devised by the agency. In either case agencies either have a flexible response to content and will make some level of change as a result of user need or the worker's judgement, or the model is seen as an off-the-shelf, tried and tested success which ought not to be altered.

Some groups are set up with the intention of continuing to be flexible in relation to activities. These are usually groups new to the agency or groups in which the stated intention is to respond to users' needs as they occur. The former are often in reality pilot groups so that workers change the intended activities once the group is in progress.

Examples of groups with pre-set activities are the Anxiety Management, the Women's Mental Health and the Male Offenders' Groups. Some variation is likely to be made in response to the worker's experience but there is a tendency for them to be viewed as an off-the-shelf product.

The Council on Addiction has produced a drug and offending group-work pack which has been used by a wide range of organizations over several years. This has a set programme of sessions and is largely used as a pre-set programme, although it has been adapted for use in prisons.

The Department of Transport-sponsored drink and drive groupwork programme, which is only provided by agencies in areas where magistrates' courts are licensed to offer this opportunity to disqualified drivers, provides a programme with the approved content. There is some flexibility since agencies may deliver it as they wish.

Within our case studies, the Male Offenders' Group fits this model well. This content has been provided by another probation service and the programme as a whole will probably be adopted by a number of services.

Groups whose function and objectives remain the same but in which the activities have some flexibility are perhaps the most common. Support groups, such as carers' groups, groups for substance misusers, people with mental health problems and wide ranges of parents' groups, fit this model. These may be open or closed groups but are often types of groups which the agency repeats in essence while changing the programme content in response to the worker's experience of previous groups and/or users' responses. Within our case studies the Positive Parenting Group and the Women's Group both fit this model.

The third approach is to set up groups which are intentionally flexible in their activities and programme contents from the outset. In our case study example, the support group for men who are main carers of young children, the worker's intention was that the members agree on, and to some extent provide, the activities themselves. How this actually worked in practice for the former group is analysed in the next section.

The case studies

What can our case studies tell us about how an actual group's activities are selected in practice? Does the leader select the goals and the activities likely to achieve these goals overtly or select the goals and appropriate activities and then try to encourage the group members to select them as their own choices? Do leaders select the group's activities even when the group has a specific ideology of self-help with only minimal worker support role? The selection of activities is a revealing window on the power relations in a group, particularly in relation to member–leader power. This is both in terms of the power of the leadership role itself, and in gendered power relationships across all aspects of members' and the leader's interactions.

The Men's Group for men who are main carers of young children

As we have seen in Chapter 2, this new open group, with only four initial members, was set up to provide support for lone male carers in an environment in which the social supports used by lone mothers were not supportive to lone fathers.

Although the group goals were set by the two workers, they felt that the group activities should be decided by the members. The selection of activities became a long process stretching over a number of group sessions. Before the group began the leaders had a number of ideas about activities, speakers, frequency of meetings and a crèche. The workers wanted the members to feel a sense of ownership and that perhaps one particular member would lead. These were all viewed as tentative assumptions by the workers.

During sessions 1 and 2 the members discussed possible activities as well as structural issues such as frequency, time and place. The latter were agreed by the end of the second session but no progress had been made on activities.

Some of the workers' assumptions had changed by this point. The members clearly were very diverse so that a broader format needed to be evolved to suit all members. The member that the workers had identified as a possible leader now seemed to be the member who was most benefiting from the support of the group.

By session 3, one of the workers decided that decisions about activities needed to be grasped. However, a number of new dimensions affected the achievement of this. A new member joined the group, which seemed to change the group dynamics. The group as a whole began a very strong criticism of women in general. This began as an analysis of their own situation in that they felt that they had been deserted by their partners and left to care for their children. This extrapolated to the domination of all women over men, and in particular to the two female workers, with their search for an agreed programme as an example of female domination. At the end of this session the workers felt the group was out of their control and unsure how to manage future sessions. The members had been deprecating woman as a whole and said that they didn't want any rules.

There was a considerable change of mood in the fourth session. The workers explained how they had felt the previous session. The members said their comments had not been aimed at the workers personally, and this led on to a very open and positive discussion about the roles of women, gender roles and the members' children. In the following session a set of rules for group discussion and some agreement on activities were achieved. This included a target to devise a leaflet to encourage more members to this open group.

There are clearly a number of interwoven gender and power issues here, which were not foreseen by the workers in their preparation processes. It seems that the sessions spent discussing appropriate activities became the core activities themselves. Clearly, the tempestuous session 3 improved relationships between workers and members and enabled them to move on to a more settled basis for the discussion of issues central to all members. This response accords well with 'fight and flight' behaviours recorded widely elsewhere in group processes (Bion 1961).

The Positive Parenting Group

This closed group with an initial membership of 12 users was essentially a model refined by this agency over a period of time. The group goals were set by the workers. These were stated as providing support to parents in identifying parenting skills in relation to child management issues. While the overall goals and means of achieving these are set by the workers, individual members can set personal goals with a worker during a home visit after the initial session. This process helps the member decide whether the group meets their needs. Parents set personal goals, such as 'deal better with temper tantrums' and 'have a clearer awareness of child developmental stages'.

The activities here are generally pre-set in that the means of achieving the group's objectives is a very wide range of task-centred exercises mostly previously used by this agency in this type of group. These may be role plays, small and large group discussions, exercises in pairs or a larger group, with feedback to the whole group, as well as home tasks.

Although the means of achieving the group goals is very clearly decided by the workers and the menu of activities is largely a given, there is an interactive process by which members' preferences are acted on. First, the specific exercises most appropriate for this particular group of members are chosen by workers in response to the members' goals discussed on the home visits. The exercises as a whole are tailored to the issues raised by each particular group of parents. In addition, at the end of each session the workers and members reflect on how successful it has been and jointly make decisions about which activities to repeat and which to drop.

This is a very successful group which fits well our model of groups which are run fairly frequently within an agency and within which the activities are agreed in advance as a broad schema, but which build in some flexibility to ensure that particular users' needs are met.

Conclusion

Although we would have to conclude from the literature and knowledge of current social groupwork that the analysis of activities is not a recognized, systematized theoretical framework in widespread use, it is clear that the wide range of professionals who use groupwork to improve users' quality of life reflect at length on the kinds of activity likely to achieve group goals and vigorously evaluate them in retrospect.

Contributions to this practice knowledge are varied and illustrate decades of activity analysis. Churchill (1959, p.54) says: '…in planning of every activity the effect of group interaction on each member must be considered'. In planning a group activity for young boys in a child guidance setting, she chose model aeroplane construction, since it required little necessary skill, allows those with skill to demonstrate it and demands no tool sharing. These elements related to goals for two particular boys that day. This illustrates planned activity selection and relates to several principles which Vinter's (1974) framework highlights. Troester and Darby (1976) provide a theoretical basis on several dimensions for the use of food in group settings; for example, 'Food provides an enjoyable reason for sitting and talking with children. It also can restore group feeling at the end of a session of competitive activity' (p.99). Williams et al. (1998), working with the Kingfisher Project for bereaved children, also introduce food to fulfil the same functions as Troester and Darby (1976). Priestley and Maguire's (1984) creative approaches to groupwork in a day prison provide a manual of activities designed to achieve particular ends for the participants. Wilkes and Colquhoun (1997) describe a health visitor-run group supporting parents to manage the behaviour of difficult children. A range of activities are used very flexibly. These include games for parents and children, modelling simple behavioural techniques and one-to-one work with parents. Vernelle (1994) utilizes Vinter's (1974) six dimensions framework to provide an analysis of group activities and to aid user-centred choice of group activities. Brown (1992) has now included a section on activity analysis in his latest edition which, given the influential nature of this core groupwork book, might suggest an increasing interest in this area. Occupational therapy literature provides a number of examples of research into the effects on participants of different types of activity. Nelson et al. (1988) compared two types of task groups: one set which shared tools and another which did not. Participants in the former group produced significantly more interactions between members than the groups which did not share tools. Schwartzberg, Howe and Mc Dermott (1982), in comparing task groups with activity and discussion groups, found that each offered unique opportunities for social interaction. McDermott (1988) compared the same three types of groups and concluded that task groups encouraged more social–emotional communication. Klyczek and Mann (1986) compared verbal-oriented groups with activity-oriented groups in a day care setting for psychiatric patients. They found that the clients attending the activity-oriented groups achieved four-and-a-half times more symptom reduction than clients attending the verbal-oriented groups. DeCarlo and Mann (1985) found that activity groups attained significantly higher levels of interpersonal communication skills than verbal groups.

Ward (1998) reviews a number of authors who are critical of 'off-the-shelf' programmes, many of a cognitive behavioural nature, used by probation services to reduce re-offending. These are criticized on a number of grounds but mainly because such pre-ordained structured programmes are oppressive since they provide little opportunity for a user's personal development. The likelihood of such an outcome would seem to rely more on the group worker's skill than the degree of pre-ordained structure. However, this discussion does illustrate the increasing focus on programme contents. Such programmes are seen in some of our case studies. Here, clearly, the quality of the selected activities is increasingly refined as workers learn from their use in other services or adapt the programmes to their particular group goals or users.

Chapter 7

Group Structure

There is clearly a relationship between group structures and the successful achievement of group outcomes. Issues we need to consider are: group size; duration, length and frequency of meetings; whether groups are open or closed; and group composition. Did our case study workers see these issues as important? Did they relate them to the achievement of group goals? Did they feel these dimensions were within their locus of control?

Size

The size of the group was not an issue for the Girls' Group since, if a larger number were recruited, several groups could be formed. This related to youth service policy. The ideal number for each group did not arise as an issue, since only six members were recruited. The Men's Group for men who are main carers of young children was in a similiar position, since this too was initially an open group with a small membership. The Anxiety Management Group workers had a clear initial policy that no more than 12 members could form a group. However, six to eight were seen to be the ideal number. In contrast, the Male Offenders' Group had eight members. The leaders thought 12 would be ideal, but there were pragmatic pressures to get the group started. The Positive Parenting Group workers had considered this issue from both professional and resource standpoints. The group size was agreed to be between 8 and 12. Eight parents were felt to be an ideal number to provide support to each other and have a range of needs to discuss. However, they were prepared to have up to 12 members, since they needed to have a sufficiently high number to justify having two workers. The workers felt this would be too difficult a group for one worker. The Women's Group usually settles at around ten members. However, if there were more than 15 members the structure would have to change, since it would be difficult to introduce new members and a second facilitator would be needed. It was agreed that the Anger Management Group would have no less than five and no more than ten members. This is agency practice for this type of group. The Women's Mental Health Group, which is closed but runs throughout the year, has a maximum of 12 and a minimum of three members.

Clearly, as Benson (1987) states, 'The purposes and needs of the group should determine its size' (p.27). As Vinter (1967) suggests, various sizes will produce different effects for their members and workers need to relate these to the desired outcomes of the group. He states that the worker's task is to determine the appropriate group size with reference to the specific effects desired for clients in terms of their treatment goals. He suggests that groups with more than nine members tend towards anonymity of membership, less consensus among members, lower rates of participation and higher demands for leadership abilities.

Hartford (1972) notes that large groups present a larger number of potential relationships to the member which places greater emotional demands than a small group, and that members will also respond to dyadic and triadic relationships of others in group interaction. In general, Hartford (1972) feels that the larger the group, the greater the emotional response demanded and the greater the cognitive demand to ideas, thoughts and decision.

Slater (1958) notes that in larger groups physical freedom is restricted while psychological freedom is increased. The member has less time to talk, more points of view to integrate and adapt to, and a more elaborate structure to fit into. He also notes that, in a larger group, members may withdraw from the discussion without being as conspicuous as in smaller groups.

Cartwright and Zander (1968) observe that there is a tendency in large groups for a smaller proportion of members to become central to the organization, make decisions for it and communicate to the total membership. It is probably in this sense that Vinter (1967) suggests that larger groups make higher demands on leadership abilities in trying to ensure full participation of all members. Vinter suggests that the effects likely to be created by larger groups, such as anonymity and interaction with a wider and larger number of individuals, may be desired for individuals with particular goals. It seems likely that groups for long-term patients about to leave hospital or groups for muscular dystrophy sufferers would not need to be small if part of the goals set were to encourage interaction with a variety of individuals and to explore a number of adaptions to common problems. The difficulty arises in respect to what is large and what is small. As in the question of selection criteria, practitioners suggest a need for balance between the extremes of a large group, in which a few members contribute and interact, and a small group in which members feel their every move is closely monitored and where there is little stimulation. Hartford (1972), for example, states groups must be small enough for each person to be heard and to feel the impact of the group upon their beliefs and behaviour, but not so small as to overexpose members or to provide too little stimulation.

Daste (1989) echoes this point in describing support groups for cancer patients. He says that many are too large so that members have less opportunity to participate. He suggests a starting number of no more than 10 to 12 but he feels an optimum size would be seven. Brown and Clough (1989) too are concerned with the effects of too large a group where interpersonal responses or task completion are central. 'When they get as large as eight or more members, subgroups tend to proliferate, verbally dominant members become more so, and the quieter members are increasingly likely to become silent' (p.33). They feel between five and seven members is a good size. Preston-Shoot (1987) also equates larger groups with sub-group formation.

In general, the literature and research studies seem to favour small groups for the types of groups which mainly concern this book. 'Small' can range from five to ten members, depending on the writer. Vinter (1967) states that small groups – that is, of less than nine members – tend towards high rates of member participation, greater consensus and more intensive relationships. Hare (1962) notes that several studies show greater member satisfaction in groups composed of five members. Groups of less than five complained the group was too small, demanding too much participation from each member, and groups with more than five members complained that the group was too large and their contributions were restricted. Castore (1962) investigated the relationship between the size of groups and the number of other members to whom individuals directed at least one remark, which he took as a measure of the spread of interpersonal interaction in the group. He studied 55 in-patient therapy groups which ranged in size between 5 and 20 members. The results showed a marked reduction in interactions between members when the group was larger than nine members and a second marked reduction when the group was larger than 17; the implication being that in in-patient settings, groups of five to eight members offer greater opportunity for member participation. Fatout and Rose (1995) focus on social services task groups and, like Brown and Clough (1989), suggest that as size increases, group cohesion decreases. They also suggest that the larger the group the greater the tendency to establish formal rules and regulations. Preston-Shoot (1987) warns us that small groups may also make some members feel pressurized into exposing their feelings. A therapeutic group, he suggests, should have six to eight members. For Brown (1994) the optimum size for many purposes is 'a group size of five or six members, large enough for stimulation, small enough for participation and recognition' (p.55).

In considering initial group size both Yalom (1985) and Daste (1989) suggest that it is advisable to start with a group slightly larger than the desired size to allow for absenteeism; two more than the minimum may be a reasonable estimate.

There is considerable agreement that as group size increases:

- some individuals participate less
- sub-groups form
- formal rules emerge
- consensus is more difficult
- members' contributions increase
- cohesion decreases
- the worker's role is more central

and that as group size decreases:

- more individuals participate, especially quieter ones
- clarity of group goals and their achievement is increased
- identity increases.

Duration, frequency and length

Preston-Shoot (1987) suggests that decisions about these structural issues are often pragmatic decisions made by agencies and particularly relate to staff availability as well as agency tradition and practice wisdom. Brown (1994) stresses flexibility in all these dimensions and, in common with most other writers, reminds us that each of these structural decisions needs to relate to group purposes.

The duration or expected life of a group is likely to affect its functioning in areas other than its tendency to be 'open' or 'closed', such as the degree and kind of member involvement, self-selection of members and attitude to group objectives. If the group is expected to be of short duration members may focus more rapidly on group objectives but invest less in relationships, because there is no expectation of permanency. Groups which have an expectation of permanence are likely to invest more in group relationships and in creating the kind of group structure that will be stable and lasting. This type of group is more likely to have a sense of group identity and to evolve its own norms and group traditions. The duration of a group is an important factor for the worker to consider, since it relates closely to the kind of group and individual goals the worker is hoping to achieve.

Brown (1994) cites the more recent tendency for the duration of groups to be brief and focused. This may be indicative of resourcing directives in the caring professions in general. Benson (1987), in contrast, reports his therapeutic groups for adults lasting six months and similar groups for children having a duration of nine months. However, he suggests that task-oriented groups such as social skills training groups should meet for 6 to 12 weeks.

The duration of the case study groups varied considerably. The Girls' Group, the Men's Group for men who are main carers of young children and the Women's Group were all open and therefore had no specific duration. The Anxiety Management, Male Offenders', Positive Parenting and Women's Mental Health Groups all had previously run programmes with very clearly agreed content but with very different durations. The Anxiety Management Group had eight weeks' duration, the Male Offenders' Group 18 weeks, the Positive Parenting Group 12 to 16 weeks and the Women's Mental Health Group six weeks. The reasons for these differences did not seem to be about the length of time needed to build trust or relationships, but were more to do with replicating previously used models. The Anger Management Group, a new initiative, also ran for six weeks.

The frequency of group meetings is also a factor likely to have some effect on group relationships and attainment of goals. Yalom (1975) reports that the meetings of psychotherapy groups, in his experience, vary from one to five times a week. He expresses a preference for twice-weekly meetings since he feels that when the group meets more than once weekly it increases in intensity, the meetings have more continuity, the group continues to work through issues raised at the previous meeting, and the entire process takes on the character of a continuous meeting. Hartford (1972) suggests that the frequency of meetings may be determined by the urgency of the problem and the level of members' concern. She, like Benson (1987), suggests that crisis intervention groups may meet from three to five times a week during the crisis. It could also be suggested that in open-ended groups, where the turnover is rapid, frequent meetings could help retain some continuity of participation.

The case study groups all met weekly except the Girls' Group. This was due to agency policy in that the service could not be provided more frequently until the need for this was proven. The workers who initiated the Men's Group wanted monthly meetings but the group members wanted to meet weekly.

Hartford (1972) and Yalom (1975) agree that the length of a session should in general be about one hour for psychotherapy or where there is a degree of emotional tension. Yalom (1975) notes that there is general consensus among therapists that after two hours a point of diminishing returns is reached and the group becomes tired and inefficient. Benson (1987), however, suggests three-hour sessions for therapy groups and two to two-and-a-half hours for task groups. He encourages us not to 'be afraid to experiment with length of sessions…to suit your group needs' (p.29). Preston-Shoot's (1987) advice is more nearly reflected in the length of meetings of case study groups. He says that sessions are usually one-and-a-half or two hours. This dimension among the case study groups showed a much greater consensus than the other elements of structure, although the reasons for the decisions were diverse. The Girls' Group lasted two hours because this is standard for youth service group sessions. The Anxiety Management Group and the Male Offenders'

Group also had two-hour sessions. This too seemed to be for traditional reasons. The Men's Group and the Positive Parenting Group both had sessions of one-and-a-half hours. In the latter case this was related to the length of time the crèche could operate and to parents' school collecting times. The latter also affected the session length for the Men's Group. The Women's Group, like the Anger Management Group, initially had one-and-a-half hour sessions, but was continuously short of time. It now has two-hour sessions with no breaks. The Women's Mental Health Group has one-and-a-quarter hour sessions. For all groups the practitioner is likely to make decisions on length of session, based on attention span and motivation of members, the group's activity base and the type of goals set.

The time at which a group meets will be determined by the members' and the worker's availability and, in a residential or hospital setting, on the institution's regime. This is an area which needs to be considered by the worker since, if the time is not set with the needs of members as a determinant, the members may be worrying about other problems during group sessions. For example, groups for depressed mothers will need to consider whether the session finishes in time for mothers to collect their school-age children. As Fatout and Rose (1995) suggest, workers need to tailor the time of day to the potential population of group members; evenings may be best for people at work and school finishing times need to be kept in mind. Clearly two out of our case study groups took this into account. Fatout and Rose (1995) also draw our attention to the times other community groups are meeting. The Girls' Group needed to do this to ensure that they had sole use of the centre and that it did not clash with the general youth groups to which some of the girls might have belonged.

Open or closed?

The question of in what circumstances groups should be 'open' or 'closed' is closely related to group size. Practitioners are not always able to determine the initial size of a group but, if it is an open group, as members drop out or others are added opportunities arise for deliberately influencing the size of the group.

If a group is ongoing, and may exist for years but with a changing membership, then there is not a possibility of it being a closed group. The salient question then becomes, how often ought new members to be added, since group identity may be lost and a feeling of instability may arise if the turnover is rapid or in large blocks. The open group, however, does provide an opportunity to increase the compatibility of members by selecting new members once the personality balance within the group has been established. New members may also bring new interpretations, ideas and values, thereby providing greater stimulus to a group.

However, a group which is intended to have a short life and whose group and individual goals are thought to be best achieved through fairly intense and stable relationships within the group will probably decide to form a closed group. This would ensure continuity of membership and group development, and encourage feelings of trust and security through which group goals might be achieved. Groups, however, which begin as closed groups may have to add extra members if so many initial members are lost that the remaining members no longer function as a group.

Douglas (1995) reminds us that groups may change over time. They may begin as closed, leader-directed groups and become open and self-directed. He states that 'all defining factors of a group are interrelated ...change to one...will have some effect on the others without exception' (p.27). Brown and Clough (1989), contrasting the differences between open and closed groups, suggest that the salient difference is changing membership and that open groups present a very broad range of types of group. These can in fact have fairly stable group membership over time or can be drop-in groups in which membership may change substantially or completely over a very short time. In residential or day-care settings, they suggest many groups may appear to be open but they may in fact be closed because 'everyone knows who belongs' (p.35). Brown and Clough (1989) describe the processes of reforming which occurs every time the membership changes. The group does not necessarily begin again, but the group dynamics will change in response to the membership changes. This process is well illustrated by the Men's Group for men who are main carers of young children which admitted a new member in week 3. This seemed to change the group dynamics, since the group then began to strongly criticize women in general (see Chapter 3). Benson (1987) calls these adaptions 'constant modifications of group culture' (p.30). He suggests that open groups can be more creative and provide, with changing membership, a greater variety of skills and personal resources. However, he thinks they can also be less predictable and lack the depth of a closed group. He sees closed groups as more consistent and cohesive, but less able to deal with change. The Women's Group, however, has a constantly changing membership. The group has evolved a process whereby the introduction of new members has become part of the group activities (see Chapter 2).

Preston-Shoot (1987) relates these dimensions to 'fit for purpose'. He suggests that task groups are more likely to need the stability of having closed membership while other groups, such as community and tenants' groups, are naturally more fluid so that their membership changes over time. He, too, sees closed groups as likely to build trust more easily, and the probability that where members have similiar needs or problems they will become a cohesive group more quickly. He is concerned that small closed groups may become unviable if some members leave. Daste (1989). in designing groups for cancer patients, suggests a compromise between open and closed structures – 'an open group which stresses attendance' (p.63). Members are often too ill to attend every session or are finding it difficult to deal with painful feelings in the group at that particular time.

Group composition

Preston-Shoot (1987) describes group composition as an 'intricate exercise' and Vinter (1967) notes that selection of group members is one of the most problematic aspects of practice with groups. Group composition, in fact, may not be an appropriate worker activity, or group composition decisions may often be outside the worker's control. For most of the case study groups, some element of group composition was within the control of the workers.

Most writers, in considering the complex issues around group composition, are concerned with the balance between 'homogeneity' and 'heterogeneity'. The former is equated with composing groups of similar people or people with similar problems or tasks, while the latter is equated with broad ranges of people and different types of issues. These two categories are seen by Brown (1994), for example, as, in broad terms, providing the worker with the choice of stability and support for members, or forces for change. Preston-Shoot (1987) suggests that we should not confuse similarity of problem with similar approaches to dealing with them. Thus many successful groups are run for people with common problems but who have a very varied range of strategies for coping with them. However, as the group worker is faced with a plethora of variables related to potential members, these twin concepts alone may not provide the worker with sufficient guidance.

Many writers (Brown 1994; Northern 1969; Preston-Shoot 1987) consider that the prime determinant of group composition should be that the needs and goals of prospective members can be met through the group's aims. This approach stresses the selection of members according to the group's prime purpose so that the group's focus is related to common concerns, capacities and shared experiences. Thus a group designed to help the personal adjustment of mothers with severely handicapped young babies would select mothers in this situation. However, given a large number of mothers in this situation, the group goals and purposes highlight a category of potential members but do not specify the particular attributes or characteristics needed to select members from the general category. Daste (1989), who runs groups for cancer patients and their relatives, finds that using prime purpose as a criterion still poses problems as to whether patients alone should be included or their relatives also.

While problem or task classification is acceptable as the prime criterion for selection, other sets of criteria will be needed in addition, if workers are seeking to compose groups which will have the greatest impact or change effects for group members. This is well illustrated by the Positive Parenting Group. Here, five members self-selected and seven members were referred by agencies. The main selection criterion was that all the parents wanted help with their parenting skills. The workers assumed that the parents would have similar issues to discuss, which in fact was the case. This is also well illustrated by the Women's Mental Health Group in which members want to work on similiar mental health issues.

In refining the group composition process beyond prime purpose, many writers (Brown 1994; Brown and Clough 1989; Douglas 1995; Fatout and Rose 1995; Preston-Shoot 1987) introduce descriptive and behavioural dimensions.

For Preston-Shoot (1987), descriptive dimensions such as age, gender, marital status, ethnicity, occupation, and so on are to be decided by the worker in terms of which are essential or desirable characteristics in relation to the group's objectives. In the case study groups, only some of these were of any concern. The Girls' Group was only concerned with gender and age. The Anxiety Management Group workers were only concerned that members did not feel isolated; for example, if the group only had one man or one woman member. In the Male Offenders' Group and the Men's Group for men who are main carers of young children, the only descriptive elements to be considered were gender.

While the behavioural dimension is mentioned by most writers as an important element of group composition in terms of likely members' behaviour, few acknowledge the complexity of establishing this. Brown and Clough (1989) suggest group workers should consider compatible behavioural attitudes of members. Fatout and Rose (1995), in considering how to motivate members of task groups, also suggest that personality of members is an issue in relation to their potential to become 'valuable, co-operative functioning members of a task group' (p.44).

There are, however, few selection methods which attempt to predict dimensions of an individual's behaviour with others. Hartford (1972) states that the behaviour tendencies which a person may show on an individual basis when tested alone may be different from actual behaviour when in the presence of others or interacting with them. Yalom (1975) suggests that, of all the prediction methods, the traditional intake individual interview appears to be the least accurate and yet the most commonly used. He therefore suggests gaining data about the patient's behaviour in a group setting by observing behaviour in a group as similar as possible, in terms of composition, task, norms and expected role behaviour, to the group.

Yalom (1975) suggests that the more similar the intake procedure is to the actual group situation, the more accurate will be the prediction of the individual's group behaviour, and that if groups of those on the waiting list are not possible, then 'simulated' groups or 'interpersonally orientated initial interviews' can be substituted. During a simulated group the subject listens to a tape recording or film of a simulated group meeting. The potential member is asked at various points what she or he feels is happening in the group, what they would do in the group or what their emotional response is.

An interpersonally orientated interview is proposed as being less accurate than waiting list groups as a means of gaining predictive data but more accessible. Here the subject is questioned about interpersonal and group relationships, early friendships and closest prolonged friendships.

Attention is also focused on the interviewee's ability to comment on the process of the interview or to accept the therapist's commentary. Yalom (1975) accepts that the validity of this type of interview has yet to be determined but feels it to be more relevant to subsequent group behaviour than traditional intake interviews. Few group workers would have the resources to operate such selection systems but Yalom (1975) does highlight issues that do not seem to be considered in those situations where some form of selection is in place.

Preston-Shoot (1987) suggests two means of selection: a referral form and a pre-meeting. The referral form would be different for each group. It would ask the potential member such questions as, 'What skills and abilities would you have to offer the group?; 'What do you think are your main difficulties?' Preston-Shoot thinks this referral form helps workers and members have clarity about group and individual goals. At this stage potential members can exclude themselves. He additionally suggests pre-group interviews for two-way clarification and a meeting with other potential members. Williams *et al.* (1998), considering preparation purposes for a group for children coping with loss, use a range of data elements as part of the selection process: referral forms, family profiles and a questionnaire completed by the child on the home visit. Information collected may also include a young people's questionnaire, a questionnaire to be completed by the professional referrer and a questionnaire to be completed by the class teacher. Clearly, although contributing to the selection process, this wide-ranging data collection serves other purposes such as providing detailed information on the child's needs to inform group processes.

Few of the case study groups attempted, or perhaps saw any need, to provide any formal selection processes. Four of the groups, however, were concerned about likely group behaviour. The Anger Management Group focused on whether potential members would interact in the group and bring energy and enthusiasm to the tasks. It is not clear how this was assessed as some of these members would be new to the agency. The Anxiety Management Group, the Male Offenders' Group and the Women's Group had various formal processes to assess likely group behaviour and group suitability.

The Anxiety Management Group workers, having a list of both self- and agency referrals, visited each potential member and completed a questionnaire. This focused on the member's motivation to bring about some personal change via the group. Issues of likely group behaviour were only relevant if the member's behaviour was likely to disrupt the group. The Male Offenders' Group used the ACE assessment format to assess members' motivation, level of risk and likely group behaviour. This is a complex questionnaire processed by the probation service. The Women's Group were concerned to gather information about the potential member's possible history of disruptive behaviour in groups. Potential members were also invited to an individual pre-meeting to assess whether they were at the right stage to benefit from the group. The Women's Mental Health Group had similiar concerns. All members are assessed on arrival at the day hospital so that group workers have the information provided by the assessment and some from outside sources.

The question of whether there can or should be any element of selection at all is raised by Preston-Shoot (1987) and Brown (1994). Brown reminds us that self-help groups may well select their own members, either by setting particular criteria or by accepting or rejecting individual potential members. He also cites criteria that relate to agency function or where group membership is determined by a court or supervision order, as in the probation service. The membership for open groups is often determined by the setting. A group for parents of children with cystic fibrosis in a hospital outpatients' department will have its membership determined by hospital appointment dates and will usually therefore be an open group. Preston-Shoot (1987) expresses reservations about selecting group members and has to some extent devised his referral form, with its potential for prospective members to self-exclude, as a means of sharing the responsibility of selection between members and workers.

Brown and Clough (1989) focus on groups in residential and day-care settings. Here, they suggest the group will be affected by the complexity of status and relationships in the setting as a whole, and in particular recent events. 'The composition of each group and groupings will therefore result in group dynamics influenced by the centre environment, as well as the group itself' (p.32).

The present state of knowledge available from research studies and contributions from the literature do not provide the group practitioner with definitive conclusions about the basis of membership selection for particular group purposes, where this is appropriate. However, the salient areas of consideration would seem to be: homogeneity/heterogeneity, prime purpose, descriptive dimensions, behavioural dimensions, selection methods and settings differences. Clearly, some contributions have been made which provide alternatives to consider in planning and this may be a basis for thoughtful consideration in the process of group composition.

Chapter 8

Conclusion

The previous chapters illustrate the range and depths of tasks which need to be considered by group workers before a group begins. Clearly, the practitioner must balance a complexity of interactive elements in this initial planning phase. While groupwork literature is available to the practitioner to aid these processes, experienced group workers also evolve practice wisdom of their own on which to draw when particular decisions need to be made.

The planned termination of the group has not been considered here, but if the group is not to be open and continuous for the foreseeable future the termination process must be determined before the group begins. Douglas (1976) provides an excellent chapter on the issues which ought to be considered in this area. The methods of evaluating the group also need to be agreed before the start of the group. This will be discussed later in this section.

Group workers work within an agency context, a societal context and sometimes within a particular professional context. In many senses the relevance of agency policy ought to have been included before any other topic. Most groups exist within an agency context. They exist only with agency agreement and resources, and can operate only within agency policy. Given this macro-framework, acceptable group purposes will also need to fit demonstrably agency policy. Benson (1987) suggests that workers should identify the agency's operational concerns and priorities for group members. This will be particularly important if all members are the agency's users. Brown (1994) suggests that workers should be aware of funding for particular user groups within the agency so that they can demonstrate the utility of their groupwork in achieving the designated purposes.

Preston-Shoot (1987) reminds us that the difficulties that group members are experiencing should not become the focus for personal pathology. Individual difficulties need to be viewed within their political, economic and social context. Group workers need to be able to conceptualize their group members within their wider social-structural context. Evidence both from the case study groups and the literature suggests that practitioners are aware of these constructs and their effects on members' lives. Donnelly's (1986) work with women on a housing estate experiencing powerlessness is a good illustration. The Girls' Group's workers' considerations of the effects on young women of living in a red light district is also a good example. Societal attitudes to male lone carers of young children encouraged two of the case study social services workers to offer them a specific group.

Agencies as employers of practitioners, and as implementers of agency policy and selectors of appropriate strategies, have profound effects on groupwork. The likelihood of a particular agency encouraging the use of groupwork depends on a number of variables. Primarily an agency needs to view groupwork as promoting its main, or at least salient, purposes. Groupwork needs to be seen as an effective use of staff time and needs to accord with the agency traditions and public image.

Whether agencies promote groupwork and the type of groups run by agencies also depends on their value base and that of their practitioners. Essentially this relates to agency/practitioner attitudes to members. These can be viewed as a continuum from individual pathology to social-structural causal factors in that the users' difficulties can be seen as emanating from problems which they or their family have created or, at the other end of the continuum, their difficulties are seen as emanating from factors created by elements within the social structure, such as the benefits system, the legal system, the education system and the employment climate. A related value element is the degree to which group members are seen to be able to take responsibility for solving their own difficulties. Preston-Shoot (1987) suggests that group members have knowledge, skills and abilities to offer each other and that practitioners need to ensure that they do not devalue or ignore members' contributions. Such a lack of acknowledgement, he feels, leads to perceptions that members are passive recipients of a groupwork experience arranged by the workers. Expectations that members are a central part of the problem-solving process are embodied in the concept of empowerment discussed in Chapter 3. Preston-Shoot (1987) feels that clients have a capacity to understand their own needs and to choose from a range of possible options.

Some groupwork evaluation systems are grounded in the value base of user empowerment and user satisfaction. This type of group evaluation in terms of its process may not differ from other group evaluation processes. It is the intention and use to which it is put that set it apart. In a number of studies group members' views of the effectiveness of particular group structures and groupwork methods were elicited. The purpose of these studies, which tend to view members as consumers, is to respond to client ratings by changing how the groups are organized. This process thus gives validity to consumer feedback by valuing clients' views. Lloyd and Maas (1997) state that 'client feedback assists service providers in determining whether clients feel that their needs have been met by the service that was provided' (p.229). Falk-Kessler, Momich and Perel (1991) examined the therapeutic factors in occupational therapy groups that clients perceived as helpful. They found these elements to be interpersonal learning, group cohesiveness and hope. Vaughan and Prechner (1985) asked psychiatric clients which groups they found most beneficial. They viewed activity groups more favourably than psycho-therapy groups. Similarly Cole and Greene (1988) found that their users preferred task-focused groups to unstructured psychotherapy groups. Webster and Schwartzberg (1992) conducted studies to determine what participants valued in occupational therapy groups.

Evaluation processes are clearly in place to serve a number of purposes which would include both users' and workers' purposes. Many agencies and professionals operate evaluation processes as part of their quality assurance systems. These groupwork processes then form part of the general quality structures operated by the caring professions. These are well illustrated by Williams et al.'s (1998) Kingfisher groupwork project for bereaved children. This thorough set of evaluation processes consisted of information collected during and after the group. During the group information was collected each week by the group observer and a group leader. After the group the children completed evaluation sheets, the children's teachers and professional referrers completed follow-up questionnaires, and parents completed an evaluation. Similar groups, the

Northampton Project (Pennells and Smith 1995) and Winstone's Wish (Stokes and Crossley 1995), which are the largest and most well-established children's bereavement projects in Britain, have also instigated very thorough evaluation systems. Many group workers design their own evaluation systems to meet the particular needs of each group. These sometimes evaluate each session or are designed to evaluate the whole life of the group. Douglas (1976, 1991) provides a range of useful evaluative formats to suit a number of purposes.

Groupwork can be a very powerful tool for workers in human services settings, and it is clear from the literature drawn from a number of disciplines that practitioners view groupwork as a medium for change. This change may be societal rather than personal and the resultant groups span a tremendous variety, from very structured time-limited groups focused on personal change to informal neighbourhood self-help groups concerned with a single campaign issue.

This book has attempted to focus on some of the main elements which group workers need to consider before starting a group. The overall perception is one of many complex elements, of group structure, leadership styles, activities, processes and dynamics, all of which interact to provide a unique product. Is it possible to extrapolate the most salient elements and the structures which contribute to their existence? Simplification of a set of complex processes is probably not particularly helpful to practitioners, but some elements are of particularly significance in determining the unique qualities of any group. Certainly the value base of the host agency and that of group workers has perhaps the strongest influence on the main purpose for which it is initiated and for whom. How this purpose is translated into a particular structured response will depend mainly on the theoretical frameworks of both the agency and, perhaps even more importantly, the group workers. For example, one agency wanting to set up a group for people with substance misuse problems may provide their workers as consultants to encourage the formation of a self-help group, while another agency may set up a time-limited, closed, formally structured group organized and led by their agency workers. The third most salient feature of any group is the group's activities or programme. To a great extent the value bases of the main players and the agreed theoretical framework will in themselves dictate many features of the group's activities. For example, in the first situation the two above agencies may encourage a self-directed approach with a user-decided programme, while the second agency may select a behavioural 'off-the-shelf' format, previously used by this or another agency.

It seems likely that the more group workers understand the underlying factors that shape groupwork outcomes, the more able they are to influence positive groupwork experience for members.

References

Abu-Ghazzeh, T. (1999) 'Housing layout, social interaction, and the place of contact in Abu-Nuseir, Jordan.' *Journal of Environmental Psychology 19*, 1, 41–73.

Ainsworth, F. and Fulcher, L. (1981) *Group Care for Children*. London: Tavistock.

Argyle, M. (1981) *Social Skills and Work*. London: Methuen.

Atkinson, K. and Wells, C. (2000) *Creative Therapies*. Cheltenham: Stanley Thornes.

Becket, A. and Rutan, J. (1990) 'Treating persons with ARC and AIDS in group psychotherapy.' *International Journal of Group Psychotherapy 40*, 19–29.

Benson, J. (1987) *Working Creatively with Groups*. London: Tavistock.

Bion, W. (1961) *Experiences in Groups and Other Papers*. London: Tavistock.

Blauner, R. (1963) *Alienation and Freedom: The Manual Worker in Industry*. Chicago: Chicago University Press.

Boer, A. and Lanz, J. (1974) 'Adolescent group therapy membership selection.' *Clinical Social Work Journal 2*, 3, 172–181.

Borman, E. (1990) *Small Group Communication Theory and Practice*. London: Harper & Row.

Brandes, D. and Phillips, H. (1977) *Gamsters' Handbook: 140 Games for Teachers and Group Leaders*. London: Hutchinson.

Braye, S. and Preston-Shoot, M. (1995) *Empowering Practice in Social Care*. Buckingham: Open University Press.

Brown, A. (1979) *Groupwork*. Aldershot: Gower.

Brown, A. (1992) *Groupwork*. 3rd edn. Aldershot: Ashgate.

Brown, A. (1994) *Groupwork*. London: Ashgate.

Brown, A. and Caddick, B. (1986) 'Models of social groupwork in Britain: a further note.' *British Journal of Social Work 16*, 1, 99–103.

Brown, A. and Clough, R. (eds) (1989) *Groups and Groupings*. London: Tavistock/Routledge.

Butler, S. and Wintram, C. (1991) *Feminist Groupwork*. London: Sage.

Canter, D. (1974) *Psychology and the Built Enviroment*. London: Architectural Press.

Cantor, D. (1991) 'Understanding, assessing, and acting in places: is an integrative framework possible?' In T. Gaerling and G. Evans (eds) *Environment, Cognition, and Action: An Integrated Approach*. New York: Oxford University Press.

Cartwright, D. and Sander, A. (1968) 'Group Dynamics.' Cited in M. Hartford (1972) *Groups in Social Work*. New York: Columbia University Press

Castore, G. (1962) 'Number of verbal inter-relationships as a determinant of group size.' In I. Yalom (1975) *The Theory and Practice of Group Psychotherapy*. New York: Basic Books.

Cave, S. (1998) *Applying Psychology to the Environment*. London: Hodder & Stoughton.

Churchill, S. (1959) 'Prestructuring group content.' *Social Work*, 4 July, 52–59.

Cole, M. (1999) *Group Dynamics in Occupational Therapy*. New Jersey: Slack.

Cole, M. and Greene, L. (1988) 'A preference for activity: a comparative study of psychotherapy groups vs occupational therapy groups for psychotic and borderline inpatients.' *Occupational Therapy in Mental Health 8*, 53–67.

Cooper, C. (1986) *Improving Interpersonal Relations: Some Approaches to Social Skills Training*. London: Gower.

Coulshed, V. and Orme, J. (1998) *Social Work Practice: An Introduction.* Basingstoke: Macmillan.

Daste, B. (1989) 'Designing Cancer Groups for Maximum Effectiveness.' *Groupwork 2*, 1, 58–69.

Davies, B. (1975) *The Use of Groups in Social Work Practice.* London: Routledge & Kegan Paul.

Davis, L. and Proctor, E. (1989) *Race Gender and Class.* New Jersey: Prentice-Hall.

DeCarlo, J. and Mann, W. (1985) 'The effectiveness of verbal versus activity groups in improving self-perceptions in interpersonal communication skills.' *American Journal of Occupational Therapy 39*, 20–27.

Doel, M. and Marsh, P. (1992) *Task-Centred Social Work.* Aldershot: Ashgate.

Dominelli, L. (1997) *Anti-Racist Social Work.* Basingstoke: Macmillan.

Donnelly, A. (1986) *Feminist Social Work with a Women's Group.* Social Work Monographs 41. Norwich: University of East Anglia.

Douglas, T. (1970) *A Decade of Small Group Theory 1960–70.* London: Bookstall Publications.

Douglas, T. (1976) *Groupwork Practice.* London: Tavistock.

Douglas T. (1978) *Basic Groupwork.* London: Tavistock.

Douglas, T. (1983) *Groups: Understanding People Gathered Together.* London: Tavistock.

Douglas, T. (1991) *A Handbook of Common Groupwork Problems.* London: Routledge.

Douglas, T. (1995) *Survival in Groups: The Basics of Group Membership.* Buckingham: Open University Press.

Dwivedi, K. (ed) (1993) *Group Work with Children and Adolescents.* London: Jessica Kingsley Publishers.

Egan, G. (1994) *The Skilled Helper.* California: Brooks/Cole.

Falk-Kessler, J., Momich, C. and Perel, S. (1991) 'Therapeutic factors in occupational groups.' *American Journal of Occupational Therapy 45*, 59–66.

Fatout, M. and Rose, S. (1995) *Task Groups in the Social Services.* London: Sage.

Finlay, L. (1993) *Groupwork in Occupational Therapy.* London: Chapman Hall.

Fletcher, B.A. (1970) *Students of Outward Bound Schools in Great Britain: A Follow-Up Study.* Bristol: University of Bristol School of Education.

Fuhrer, U., Kaiser, F. and Hartig, T. (1993) 'Place attachment and mobility during leisure time.' *Journal of Environmental Psychology 13*, 4, 309–321.

Fulcher, L. and Ainsworth, F. (1985) *Group Care Practice.* London: Tavistock.

Giddens, A. (1987) *Social Theory and Modern Sociology.* Oxford: Blackwell.

Garvin, C. (1974) 'Task centred group work.' *Social Service Review 48*, 4, 494–507.

Gifford, R. (1987) *Environmental Psychology: Principles and Practice.* Massachusetts: Alleyn and Bacon.

Gump, P. V. and Sutton-Smith, B. (1955) 'Activity setting and social interaction: A field study.' *American Journal of Orthopsychiatry 25*, October, 755–760.

Gutheil, I. (1992) 'Considering the physical environment: An essential component of good practice.' *Social Work 37*, 5, 391–396.

Habermann, U. (1990) 'Self Help Groups: A Minefield For Professionals' *Groupwork 3*, 3, 221–235.

Hall, A. (1974) *The Point of Entry.* London: Allen and Unwin.

Ham-Rawbottom, K., Gifford, R. and Kelly, T. (1999) 'Defensible space theory and the police: Assessing the vulnerability of residences to burglary.' *Journal of Environmental Psychology 19*, 2, 117–129.

Hare, A. (1962) *Handbook of Small Group Research.* New York: The Free Press.

Harris, V. (1994) *Community Work Skills Manual Section 8.* Newcastle: Access Community Work.

Hartford, M. (1972) *Groups in Social Work.* New York: Columbia University Press.

Haywood, D., Rothenberg, M. and Bersley, P. (1974) 'Children's play and urban playground environments: A comparision of traditional, contemporary and adventure playground types.' *Environment and Behavior 6*, 131–168.

Heap, K. (1979) *Process and Action in Social Work with Groups.* Oxford: Pergamon Press.

Heap, K. (1985) *The Practice of Social Work with Groups: A Systematic Approach.* London: Allen & Unwin.

Hickson, A. (1995) *Creative Action Methods.* Bicester: Winslow.

Houston, G. (1990) *The Red Book of Groups.* London: The Rochester Foundation.

Hunter, D., Bailey, A. and Taylor, B. (1996) *The Facilitation of Groups.* Aldershot: Gower.

Hunter, D. (1992) *The Zen of Groups: A Handbook for People Meeting with a Purpose.* Aldershot: Gower.

Johnson, D. and Johnson, F. (1987) *Joining Together, Group Theory and Group Skills.* New Jersey: Prentice-Hall.

Kamya, H. (1997) 'Groupwork with children from HIV/AIDS-affected families.' *Journal of HIV/AIDS Prevention and Education for Adolescents and Children 1,* 2, 73–91.

Kerr, J. and Tacon, P. (1999) 'Psychological responses to different types of locations and activities.' *Journal of Environmental Psychology 19,* 3, 287–294.

Klyczek, J. and Mann, W. (1986) 'Therapeutic modality comparisons in day treatment.' *American Journal of Occupational Therapy 40,* 606–611.

Konopka, G. (1963) *Social Group Work: A Helping Process.* New Jersey: Prentice-Hall.

Kuenstler, P. (ed) (1954) *Social Groupwork in Great Britain.* London: Faber & Faber.

Langan, M. and Day, L. (1992) *Women and Social Work: Towards a Woman Centred Practice.* Basingstoke: Macmillan.

Levine, B. (1967) *Fundamentals of Group Treatment.* Worthbrook: Whitehall Company.

Lloyd, C. and Maas, F. (1997) 'Occupational Therapy group work in psychiatric settings.' *British Journal of Occupational Therapy 60,* 5, 226–230.

McDermott, A. (1988) 'The effect of three group formats on group interaction patterns.' *Occupational Therapy in Mental Health 8,* 69–89.

Mistry, T. and Brown, A. (1991) 'Black/white co-working in groupwork.' *Groupwork 4,* 2, 101–118.

Mullender, A. and Ward, D. (1991) *Self-Directed Groupwork.* London: Whiting and Birch.

Nelson, D., Perterson, C., Smith, D., Boughton, J. and Whalen, G. (1988) 'Effects of project versus parallel groups on social interaction and the affective leap cases of senior citizens.' *American Journal of Occupational Thrapy 42,* 23–29.

Nelson-Jones, R. (1986) *Human Relationship Skills.* Eastbourne: Reinehart and Winston.

Newman, O. (1972) *Defensible Space.* London: Architectural Press.

Northern, H. (1969) *Social Work with Groups.* New York: Columbia University Press.

Oseland, N. and Donald, I. (1993) 'The evaluation of space in homes: A facet study.' *Journal of Environmental Psychology 13,* 3, 251–261.

Osmond, H. (1959) 'The Relationship between Architecture and Psychiatrist.' Cited in M. Hartford (1972) *Groups in Social Work.* New York: Columbia University Press.

Parsloe, P. (1968) 'Some thoughts on social group work.' Paper given to Tavistock casework course.

Parsloe, P. (1971) 'What social workers say in groups.' *British Journal of Social Work 1,* 1, 39–62.

Pearson, G., Treseder, J. and Yelloly, M. (eds) (1988) *Social Work and the Legacy of Freud: Psychoanalysis and Its Uses.* London: Macmillan.

Peloquin, S. (1983) 'The development of an occupational therapy interview/therapy set procedure.' *American Journal of Occupational Therapy 37,* 457–461.

Pennells, M. and Smith, S. (1995) 'Creative groupwork methods with bereaved children.' In S. Smith and M. Pennells (eds) *Interventions with Bereaved Children.* London: Jessica Kingsley Publishers.

Phillips, J. C. (1989) 'Targeted Activities in Group Work.' *Groupwork 2,* 1, 48–57.

Preston-Shoot, M. (1987) *Effective Groupwork.* London: Macmillan.

Priestley, P. and Maguire, J. (1984) *Social Skills in Prison and the Community.* London: Tavistock.

Proshansky, H., Ittelson, W. and Rivlin, L. (eds) (1976) *Environmental Psychology: People and Their Physical Settings.* New York and London: Reinehart and Winston.

Reid, W.J. and Epstein, L. (1972) *Task-Centered Casework.* New York: Columbia University Press.

Rogers, C. (1992) *On Becoming a Person.* London: Constable Press.

Rutan, J. and Stone, W. (1984) *Psychodynamic Group Psychotherapy.* New York: Macmillan Publishing Company.

Schwartzberg, S., Howe, M. and McDermott, A. (1982) 'A comparison of three group formats for facilitating social interaction.' *Occupational Therpy in Mental Health 2*, 1–16.

Slater, P. (1958) 'Contrasting Correlates by Group Size.' *Sociometry 21*, 129–139.

Slater, R. and Lipman, A. (1980) 'Towards caring through design.' In R. Walton and D. Elliott (eds) *Residential Care*. Oxford: Pergamon.

Smith, P. (1974) 'Aspects of playground environment.' In D. Canter and T. Lee (eds) *Psychology and the Built Environment*. London: Architectural Press.

Sommer, R. (1969) *Personal Space*. New Jersey: Prentice-Hall.

Sommer, R., Wong, C. and Cook, E. (1992) 'The soft classroom 17 years later.' *Journal of Environmental Psychology 12*, 4, 337–343.

Stokes, J. and Crossley, D. (1995) 'Camp Winston: A residential intervention for bereaved children.' In S. Smith and M. Pennells (eds) *Interventions with Bereaved Children*. London: Jessica Kingsley Publishers.

Sutton, C. (1994) *Social Work, Community Work and Psychology*. Leicester: British Psychological Society.

Thompson, N. (1997) *Anti-Discriminatory Practice*. Basingstoke: Macmillan.

Troester, J. and Darby, J. (1976) 'The role of the mini meal in therapeutic play groups.' *Social Casework 2*, February, 97–103.

Van der Ven, K. (1985) 'Activity programming: Its developmental and therapeutic role in group care.' In L. Fulcher and F. Ainsworth (eds) *Group Care Practice with Children*. London: Tavistock.

Vaughan, P. and Prechner, M. (1985) 'Occupation or therapy in psychiatric day care?' *British Journal of Occupational Therapy 38*, 169–176.

Veitch, R. and Arkklin, D. (1995) *Environmental Psychology: An Interdisciplinary Perspective*. New Jersey: Prentice-Hall.

Vernelle, B. (1994) *Understanding and Using Groups*. London: Whiting and Birch.

Vinter, E. E. (1974) 'Program activities: An analysis of their effects on participant behaviour.' In P. Glasser, R. Savri and R. Vinter (eds) *Individual Change through Small Groups*. New York: The Free Press.

Vinter, R. D. (1967) *Readings in Groupwork Practice*. Michigan: Campus Publications.

Ward, D. (1998) 'Groupwork.' In R. Adams, L. Dominelli and M. Payne (eds) *Social Work, Themes, Issues and Critical Debates*. Basingstoke: Macmillan.

Webster, D. and Schwartzberg, S. (1992) 'Patients' perceptions of common factors in occupational therapy groups.' *Occupational Therapy in Mental Health 12*, 2–24.

Wheal, A. (1998) *Adolescence: Positive Approaches to Working with Young People*. Lyme Regis: Russell House.

Whittaker, D. (1985) *Using Groups to Help People*. London: Routledge & Kegan Paul.

Whittaker, J. K. (1974) 'Programme activities: Their selection and use in a therapeutic mileu.' In P. Glasser, R. Sarri and R. Vinter (eds) *Individual Change through Small Groups*. New York: The Free Press.

Wilkes, Z. and Colquhoun, C. (1997) 'Managing behaviour: a group supporting parents of difficult children.' *Health Visitor 70*, 417–418.

Williams, J., Chalener, J., Bean, D. and Tyler, S. (1998) 'Coping with loss: The development and evaluation of a children's bereavement project.' *Journal of Child Health Care 2*, 2, 58–65.

Wolpe, J. (1982) *The Practice of Behavioural Therapy*. New York: Pergamon Press.

Wools, R. and Canter, D. (1970) 'The effects of the meanings of buildings on behaviour.' *Applied Ergonomics 1*, 144–150.

Yalom, I. (1975, 1985) *The Theory and Practice of Group Psychotherapy*. New York: Basic Books.

Further reading

Fell, M. (1994) 'Helping older children grieve: a group therapy approach.' *Health Visitor 67*, 92–94.

Garvin, C. and Reed, B. (eds) (1983) 'Groupwork with Women/Groupwork with Men.' *Social Work with Groups 6*, 3/4 (special double issue).

Keenan, E. and Pinkerton, J. (1988) 'Social action groupwork as negotiation: Contradictions in the process of empowerment.' *Groupwork 1*, 3, 229–238.

Muston, R. and Weinstein, J. (1988) 'Race and groupwork: Some experiences in practice and training.' *Groupwork 1*, 1, 30–40.

Opie, N. D., Goodwin, T., Finke, L. M., Beattey, J. M., Lee, B. and Van Epps, J. (1992) 'The effects of a bereavement group experience on bereaved children's and adolescents' affective and somatic distress.' *Journal of Child Psychology 5*, 20–26.

Preston-Shoot, M. (1988) 'A model for evaluating groupwork.' *Groupwork 1*, 2, 147–157.

Sheik, S. (1986) 'An Asian mothers' self-help group.' In S. Ahmed, J. Cheetham and J. Small (eds) *Social Work with Black Children and Their Families.* London: Batsford.

Wilson, M. (1988) *Occupational Therapy in Short-Term Psychiatry.* Edinburgh: Churchill Livingstone.

Subject Index

Author Index